The Bank
Investor's
Handbook

Nathan Tobik

Kenneth Yellen

DEDICATION

To all prospective bank investors, may your portfolios
prosper as ours have from bank stocks.

CONTENTS

"A person of understanding delights in wisdom"
-The Bible

INTRODUCTION

Quick! Name an industry that touches people's lives on an everyday or frequent basis. Perhaps you thought of grocery stores or something sexy like internet retailing, but chances are you didn't think of banking. Yet, most likely you interact with a bank every time you're paid and when you pay your bills. Banks facilitate the flow of money through the economy and even if you don't interact with a bank daily, the businesses you deal with on a daily basis do.

For all the interaction people have with banks, few understand how they work or why they work. Even fewer understand why they should consider including bank stocks in their investment portfolio. There are a lot of myths surrounding banks, just like there are myths surrounding anything that initially appears complicated.

There are a lot of misconceptions about banks, including understanding what they are and what they do. For many people the word "bank" evokes images of receiving a toaster upon opening an account, or thoughts of security related to the storing of precious items in a safety deposit box. Others might go further and tap their inner Michael Moore and talk about how banks are greedy and evil.

Let's face it. Banks are now perennially stereotyped as

'bad guys'. They have been typecast in popular media as villains for eons. From the Christmastime favorite, "It's a Wonderful Life", to action and suspense movies with a nefarious banker executing clandestine wire transfers, banks and bankers are typically viewed by the general public as a necessary evil or, for many, just evil.

They don't pay enough on our deposits and charge too much on our loans. They foreclose on our house when we miss a payment (or two or three . . .). The Great Financial Crisis and subsequent Great Recession did not enhance the reputation for banking, instead it reinforced the view that these institutions are blood-sucking vampires that aren't viable businesses without government support.

Your co-authors have been wanting to write this book for a while. It's our belief that banks aren't just places to store idle savings (on which you receive virtually nothing in interest) or to cash checks, but that they should be an integral part of an investor's portfolio. The goal of this book is to provide you with a foundation and framework with which you can both begin to understand banks, but also learn the basic tools used to analyze banks as investments.

This book is intended for anyone who has ever wondered about banks either generally or in the context of investing. It's written for the investor who is more or less comfortable with basic financial concepts, such as the balance sheet and income statement. Don't worry, you don't need to be an expert in anything related to financials in order to get something out of this book.

That's what this book is. This book isn't the final testament on everything banking. This isn't a book for experts who wring their hands over FASB rule changes or waffle on investing in a bank due to a morsel of minutia buried in the footnotes. These aren't bad things, in fact they're good things, but experts don't need a book like this. We also firmly believe that one doesn't need to read 10 years of financials or build a 30-tab Excel chart modeling interest rate risk from 1940 to the present day in order to become a successful bank investor. That's the point of this book - to arm you with the basic tools, but not overwhelm you.

You might come away from reading this book rearing to go and excited to analyze banks. But it's also possible you might decide after reading this book that banks aren't something you want to include in your portfolio. Either result is ok with us. The goal of this book is to inform, educate and provide the framework for you to make the decision on banks as investments. We hope to make it both entertaining and enlightening.

Before we get into the meat of the book you deserve to know the background of your co-authors. Both of us have experience and exposure to the banking industry from an investment standpoint and we both share the perspective of looking at the industry as investors, not bankers. Outsiders, if you will.

YOUR CO-AUTHORS

Nathan Tobik is the Founder of Red River Research Inc., a company that specializes in building products and tools that turn data into profits.

Our flagship product is CompleteBankData (Web: http://www.completebankdata.com), a tool that takes bank related information from regulatory financials to individual mortgage records to UCC financing statements and combines them in easy to use dashboards. Looking to refi a competitor out of the market in a month? Call us!

Looking to buy a bank? We can help. Looking for actionable leads? It's what we do.

Nate also writes a popular investment blog called Oddball Stocks (http://www.oddballstocks.com) where he posts research on banks and small cap value stocks, as well as essays on market strategy.

Nate lives in suburban Pittsburgh, PA with his wife and four boys. When he isn't working he can usually be found outdoors, running, skiing, hiking, camping, or biking usually with multiple kids in tow. You can reach Nate at ntobik@completebankdata.com

Kenneth Yellen is an attorney, consultant, and private investor. As a Partner at several large law firms, Ken advised his Wall Street investment bank and hedge fund clients on billions of dollars in deals during his career. His many years of practicing finance law piqued his interest in the stock market. Ken enjoys consulting on legal and financial matters and is an avid private investor with a passion for bank stocks. Ken lives in suburban Washington, DC with his wife and two kids. In his spare time, Ken can be found listening to 80s music while Ubering his kids around town. He firmly believes that you can always watch *The Shawshank Redemption* one more time. Ken can be reached at ken@yellenconsulting.com.

1 WHAT IS A BANK?

So first things first. What is a bank?

As typical members of society most of us have had experiences with a bank on one or more levels. For some it's a matter of using a bank for a savings account and/or a checking account. Others use banks to obtain financing in order to purchase a home or a car. In fact, it's very hard for a consumer to get by in today's world without interacting with a bank in some fashion.

Even though one might have experience using a bank it doesn't mean they understand how a bank works or the role it plays. To assume such understanding would be like assuming that riding in an airplane makes one an expert on aviation.

If money is the lifeblood of an economy then banking is the heart that keeps that blood pumping. Banks in their most basic form are simply financial intermediaries that help people who have money (depositors) find people who need money (borrowers). It's obviously more complicated than that, but bear with us for a moment. It's necessary to dig the foundation of a house before one chooses the wainscoting.

Let's imagine a world without banks for a minute. To maintain our focus on simplicity we will assume this world has no institutional alternatives to banks (there are loan shark associations, but we won't go there).

In this mythical non-banking world let's pretend we own and run a small retail store. Perhaps it sells hardware, home goods or groceries. It doesn't really matter. Customers come into our shop and purchase goods with cold, hard cash since in our world without banks there are no checks, debit cards or credit cards.

Without a bank we have to keep all of the cash from each day's sales somewhere in our store. Suddenly, with this large and growing pile of cash we become a prime robbery target. So we install a safe in the back room, but we're always worried about storing our cash.

When the time comes to purchase inventory to re-stock our store we need to take cash from the safe and somehow get it safely to the vendor. Maybe we hire a courier or deliver it ourselves. It's one thing if the vendor is located in town, but it becomes quite problematic and costly if the vendor is out of the area. In addition, without cash on hand we simply can't purchase any inventory unless the vendor personally decides to extend us credit. However, the proverbial chickens will eventually come home to roost and our issues with moving cash will not disappear.

Now, let's imagine our business is successful and we decide we'd like to expand. Once again, the only way to pay for such growth is from cash on hand. We would need to save up for our expansion ahead of time or expand at a snail's pace (if that's even possible) paying workers periodically as and when money trickles in to our store.

So far we've looked at this from our perspective, but what about all of our customers who will also need to conduct business with us on a strictly cash basis? If we're selling low priced items this might be all right, but if we're selling high priced or big ticket items it might be difficult to make a sale. There aren't many people who walk around with their pockets stuffed with cash.

Finally, if the business is very successful our safe in the back room will fill up quickly and we'll want to look for ways we can invest our excess cash. We could make direct investments in other businesses or maybe even buy other businesses outright.

But say we want to run things in a more conservative manner and want some fixed income. Unless we limit ourselves to government issued bonds, without banks we need to personally find someone who is looking to borrow, evaluate their creditworthiness and manage the lending ourselves.

All of this takes significant time and effort and requires a skill set that we likely don't even have. We're running a retail store after all, not a financial institution. At the very least it will detract us from running our small shop. What would probably happen is the effort to find an acceptable investment would be too much and we'd just let the excess cash pile up earning nothing.

In short, a world without banks is inefficient. It's also risky. It places the burden of handling transactions, securing money, and facilitating investments in the hands of everyday people who in most cases aren't equipped to take proper care.

Now let's re-imagine our mythical little retail store in

the world as we know it. A world with banks.

Customers are now able to pay for merchandise with their choice of cash, checks, or debit or credit cards. We are able to pay vendors without carrying a bag of cash across town or hopping on a plane. We can get financing from our bank in the event we wish to expand.

Lastly, our money is stored safely on deposit at our bank and we no longer have to worry about securing the safe in the back room. While we keep our savings on deposit at the bank, they in turn loan it out to people looking to borrow money in exchange for a fee (i.e. interest). They in turn pay us part of the amount they receive as interest on our deposited funds.

As you can see, a bank is simply an intermediary. They are in the business of matching funds from depositors to borrowers who need financing for a purchase or other need.

TYPES OF BANKS

While all banks act as financial intermediaries in one form or another, not all of them do it in the same manner. In addition, many banks perform other functions and own related businesses (financial and otherwise). These businesses may be anything from insurance to leasing to data processing.

Banks can be broadly grouped into the following primary categories: community banks, regional banks, industrial banks and megabanks (otherwise known as money center banks). We will provide a brief description of each which is intended only to introduce the topic and not to be all encompassing.

COMMUNITY BANKS

When most people think of banks it is likely that they're thinking of community banks. These are the "local" banks that exist in everyone's neighborhood. A community bank is like the famous Bailey Bros. Building and Loan from the movie "It's a Wonderful Life". The ones where back in the day your parents (or you!) went in and got a toaster or wall calendar as a reward for opening an account.

A community bank is typically a banking institution with $1 billion dollars or less in assets, although sometimes this definition is stretched to include banks with $5 billion or even $10 billion in assets. The most common source of community bank funding is through deposits gathered through neighborhood and local branches. Their lending is typically limited to traditional residential mortgages and small business loans to local companies.

REGIONAL BANKS

A regional bank can be thought of as a community bank that has bulked up and covers a larger, but still confined, geographic area. If a community bank is akin to your local burger joint, a regional bank is the equivalent of In-N-Out Burger, Shake Shack, Jack in the Box or White Castle (it is amazing how easy it is to come up with these!). A regional bank will typically also have additional products and business lines, such as asset management and even investment banking.

Regional banks fund themselves through deposits obtained from a network of branches in the same way community banks do. There's simply more of them dispersed over a wider area.

The loan portfolios of regional banks are more diversified with a larger proportion of commercial and industrial lending. Regional banks have bigger balance sheets as compared to community banks and this gives them the ability to extend larger loans. If a business needs a $50m loan for expansion, for example, a large community bank might be able to provide it. If a business needs a $500m loan for expansion they will need to look to a regional (or even larger) bank as this would stretch the capabilities and lending limits of any community bank.

INDUSTRIAL BANKS

Industrial banks typically operate in one or more commercial niches. Continuing our burger joint analogy, an industrial bank might be thought of as something like Bobby's Burger Palace which features high end ingredients and caters to the crowd that wants a gourmet burger at a gourmet price. (And, yes, Bobby's Burger Palace is real. It was started by Food Network Star, Bobby Flay.)

Industrial banks are mostly funded through brokered deposits (i.e. deposits placed by brokers who make their decisions based on the highest interest rates offered), not branch deposits like a community or regional bank. Instead of making traditional residential or business loans, industrial banks focus their lending on one or more specific sectors. An example might be an industrial bank that provides lease financing for aircraft engines or railroad cars. One of the largest industrial banks is GE Capital.

MEGABANKS

The megabanks (also known as money center banks) of the world are the ones found everywhere. To absolutely kill an analogy, these are the McDonald's of the world. Megabanks are the ones that commonly are found in the news, such as JPMorgan, Citibank, Bank of America and Wells Fargo. There are a dozen or two of these 'scattered' around the world with several in Japan, Germany, etc. In technical banking parlance these are the banks that are deemed "systemically important" or "too big to fail".

Where assets at community banks and regional banks are generally measured in the millions and billions, respectively, the assets at megabanks are measured in the trillions. Just for point of reference, the assets of JPMorgan, Citibank, Bank of America and Wells Fargo in the aggregate are greater than the assets of the other 5,762 banks together.

Megabanks fund themselves, in part, through the same deposit mechanisms that regional and community banks do (obviously on a much larger scale), but this is where the similarities end. Megabanks essentially do just about everything that can be done from a financial standpoint. They all contain investment banking arms, as well as diversified lending operations. In any given day a megabank might underwrite an initial public offering (IPO) and a large bond offering, facilitate a multi-billion dollar merger, as well as make hundreds or thousands of residential mortgage, auto and business loans.

OTHER FINANCIAL ENTITIES

There are a whole host of other types of financial entities that perform bank-like or quasi bank-like functions. This includes everything from credit unions to investment banks to merchant banks. It is beyond the scope of this book to delve into these, any of which would require a book in their own right.

One thing that's great about banking is the principles are universal and ideas that apply to community banks also apply to merchant banks or credit unions. To some extent, all banking entities make money by finding depositors and connecting them with borrowers.

2 WHY EVERY PORTFOLIO NEEDS BANK STOCKS

The usual path to becoming an investor is when a person decides that whatever miniscule interest they're earning in a savings account at their local bank is ridiculous and insufficient. Especially in the post financial crisis years, interest in a bank account doesn't even beat the rate of inflation. Typically, the only way to grow savings at a satisfactory level is to start a business or invest in a business (either directly or indirectly via stocks).

Anyone with an idea and a bit of hard work can start a business. The simplest businesses don't require much capital or much administration, but usually aren't scalable either. They can be run by any 14 year old, such as a lawn mowing business. A high school kid mowing lawns just needs a mower, some gas and some kind and willing neighbors.

Marketing for the mowing business might consist of a few flyers distributed around the neighborhood. More than likely a small lawn mowing startup won't need much, if any, initial capital because the founder can "borrow" their parent's lawnmower and can pay for their future gas purchases out of cash flow. If the budding landscaper continues to add clients they can grow organically by hiring friends and buying additional lawnmowers out of their profits.

The story above describes in a simplistic form a large swath of American businesses. These are companies started on a shoestring and prayer and grown slowly with profits. But what happens when a business needs to scale quickly or make large equipment purchases in order to sustain growth?

A business looking for outside capital (i.e. retained earnings are insufficient) has two choices: obtain bank/debt financing or issue equity. Issuing equity to outside investors can be accomplished via an IPO or through venture financing. While IPO's and venture capital make for shiny and splashy news stories and headlines, they are not the most common way for small businesses to grow.

In the grand scheme of things very few companies engage in equity financing. A more popular method of financing a growing business is with debt. This is because equity financing is more "expensive" than debt (it is permanent and, thus, investors require a higher return) and also because debt provides tax advantages. When equity is issued the shareholders essentially become partners in the business until such time as they sell or otherwise dispose of their shares. If a business obtains a loan they have the ability, and obligation, to pay it back at some predetermined time in the future. The interest on the loan is tax deductible which reduces the company's overall tax burden.

When a small business wants to grow a typical course of action is for them to go to their local bank and ask for a business loan. The friendly guy or gal sitting at the desk near the front of the bank looks at the business's financials, evaluates the owner and the business's prospects and determines whether or not to extend a loan. A common misconception is that bank business financing is only predicated on the financial estimates for the business, however, it also hinges on the owner, the market and a host of other factors.

Business lending is very profitable for banks. Business customers are usually required to maintain a certain level of deposits at the bank that extends them the loan. This means that a business keeps their money on deposit at the bank only to have it lent right back at a higher rate. Secondly, business loans carry higher interest rates than other types of loans. This is to compensate for the elevated risk associated with business lending. Oftentimes there are no hard assets to lend against so the bank relies primarily (possibly solely) on the expected cashflows of the business to cover interest payments and eventually pay back principal. If economic conditions aren't favorable, a business, especially one with debt, can slide from being healthy to kaput quickly.

Regular public market investors don't have the opportunity to invest in the tens of thousands of small businesses that are the lifeblood of the economy. These are small businesses that provide vital services, such as mechanics, plumbers, electricians and small retail shops, among other things, yet these businesses have no public market presence.

While the public securities markets consist of thousands upon thousands of traded equities, most public companies are not like the type of small businesses we've been discussing. It's pretty rare, for example, to call up say Bob & Son's Plumbing and have Bob (who else?) tell you he can't fix your toilet that's on the fritz because he will be ringing the opening bell at the NYSE. This is because there are tons of hoops to jump through in order to be a public company. It's very expensive and a public company needs to comply with SEC regulations, hire auditors to publish financial statements and pay exchange listing fees. The burden to be a small listed company is approximately $250,000 per year at a minimum. For millions of small businesses the $250,000 price to ride the public markets rollercoaster is multiples of their yearly net income or even revenue.

There are over 18 million companies in the US and over 10 million of them have less than 25 employees. Out of these 10 million companies only a small fraction of a percent have a public market listing. Yet, these unlisted companies provide essential services and functions to the economy. The question for an investor is: "how does one gain exposure to such a large cross section of the economy if these businesses don't have any publicly traded equities?"

By investing in a bank of course! (You knew it all the time, although the title of this book may have provided a good hint). Investing in a bank, especially a community bank, is a backdoor investment into some of the smallest businesses in the country. On the flip side, an investment in a regional or megabank can give an investor exposure to larger private companies.

When a bank makes a loan to a business they are gaining exposure to this business (in Wall Street parlance, they are economically "long" the business). If the business does well the bank will receive their principal back together with interest. The interest is compensation for taking on the risk of extending the loan. In many cases, the interest rate on a business loan is equal to the profit margin the business is able to generate. That is, a loan might carry a 6% interest rate and a small plumbing supply company might earn a 6% net profit. What this means for a bank is their share of the company's earnings can be equal to what the owner themselves might make from owning the company. In other words a fixed exposure through a bank can give a similar level of access to profits that would be possible via equity ownership.

A bank can be thought of as a company that makes a variety of investments in businesses at fixed or semi-fixed rates. For a small bank these are investments in mostly small local businesses. Regional banks invest in midsized firms in multiple localities and national banks are a proxy for investing in the economy as a whole due to their large reach and footprint.

Investors who wish to gain exposure to segments of the economy that don't generally have any kind of corresponding traded securities can do so by investing in banks that make loans to those segments of the economy.

Each bank has a specific market focus and an investment in a bank's common stock gives an investor exposure to that segment or segments of the market. If a bank is located in an area dominated by agriculture the bank will almost certainly be overly exposed to agricultural lending or lending to residential borrowers whose jobs depend on agriculture.

An investment in a bank is a proxy for investing capital into and gaining exposure to the results of local businesses (or larger businesses depending on the size of the bank). These are businesses that don't trade on any exchange and sometimes zig when the economy is zagging.

Smaller banks are more concentrated in their exposure to local economies. For this reason it's wise to diversify geographically the banks you purchase for your portfolio.

3 HOW DOES A BANK WORK?

How does a bank work? How do they make money? What is it that they even do? These are all good questions which deserve answers so now, let's delve a little deeper into the inner workings of a bank.

The easiest way to explain how a bank works is by once again entering the world of make-believe and describing a fictitious bank. Let's imagine that a group of friends decide they want to open a business together and agree to start a small bank. They've heard banking can be lucrative and want a piece of the pie. They would like to move on up and get a deluxe apartment in the sky.

After obtaining all the necessary approvals from regulators (not easy in the least, but for purposes of our mythical bank we will assume it's done), the group is ready to jump into the wonderful world of banking. "Come in," other bankers tell them, "the water is fine!" They even have a name, '3-6-3 Bank', a reference to the days when bankers paid 3% on deposits, loaned the money out at 6% and then left to hit the links by 3pm. Each of the five friends contributes $2,000 towards starting 3-6-3 Bank. Together, their initial investment is $10,000 and this constitutes the initial bank capital.

The friends want to keep their startup expenses to a

minimum and thankfully each partner has a specific skill set to contribute towards getting 3-6-3 Bank off the ground. One is a lawyer who drafts the organizational documents. Another is a local real estate expert. The others are an IT guru, a credit analyst and an operations manager, respectively. With a lot of sweat equity and their skills and funds pooled they are able to form their bank with only $2,000 in expenses, leaving them $8,000 as capital.

Banks are all regulated by one or more regulators and 3-6-3 Bank is no exception (remember it was noted above that our five friends needed to get regulatory approval). Among countless other things, the bank is required to hold 8% of the value of their assets in capital in order to be considered 'well-capitalized'. Bank capital is a buffer against losses and provides the bank with liquidity. With $8,000 in capital the bank can potentially loan out up to $100,000 to customers.

Even though the bank can loan up to $100,000 with their $8,000 in capital, they still need the money to loan. Funds for loans don't magically materialize, they have to come from somewhere. Since the five founders have already committed $2,000 apiece they don't want to contribute another $18,400 each in order to get to the $100,000 they need ($8,000 in initial capital + $18,400 each ($92,000) = $100,000). In order to fund themselves they decide to seek customer deposits, the cheapest source of funding available to them.

The bank opens a small branch, runs some clever and poignant ads with a catchy jingle ("3-6-3. . . here for you and me!") and is successful in attracting $100,000 in deposits. Because the bank is small the only account they can offer is a standard savings account. And because they're a new bank that's working hard to attract deposits they have to pay 1% to depositors in order to attract the funds.

The bank's customer deposits are considered a liability, which at first seems strange. The bank has $8,000 in capital and $100,000 in deposits, but no assets. Their deposits are a liability because customers can ask for their money back at any time and the bank is obligated to comply.

Financial statements always need to be balanced between assets and liabilities. What this means is that the bank's $100,000 in deposits are recorded as a liability, while the actual cash they provide to the bank is considered an asset.

It's interesting to note that in a commonsensical kind of way banks are sort of backwards in terms of what assets and liabilities are. Loans that a bank makes are assets, while deposits (which must of course be returned at some point, at least in theory) are liabilities. It is often said that a good, core group of deposits is actually an asset, while loans are liabilities.

At this point the bank has $108,000 in cash as an asset and $100,000 in deposits as a liability. You'll notice that the asset and liabilities aren't equal, this $8,000 difference is the bank's equity capital.

The bank's 1% interest rate on deposits means they're now committed to paying $1,000 a year to depositors. To fund this the bank needs to put their $100,000 in deposits to work. They could buy treasuries, for example, but the return on them these days is paltry. So they decide their best course of action is to make some loans.

3-6-3 Bank had so much success with advertising for

deposits they decide to advertise their availability to make loans. Since there isn't much capital to work with the bank is restricted to making smaller loans. From both a regulatory and risk management standpoint they can't allow any one loan to dominate their balance sheet. The friends decide that they don't want any loan to exceed $5,000, meaning they'll have at least 20 borrowers, if not more.

As they did with their deposits the bank will have to offer an appealing rate in order to attract borrowers. This is because 3-6-3 Bank is new and has no brand recognition in the area they serve.

Their campaign is a success and they end up extending $100,000 in short term loans to borrowers at a 5% interest rate. These loans mature in under a year on average giving the bank some liquidity as they are repaid and roll off.

If we were to create a simple balance sheet for 3-6-3 Bank it would look like the table on the following page.

Assets

Cash	$8,000
Loans to 20 borrowers	$100,000
Total Assets	$108,000

Liabilities

Deposits	$100,000
Total Liabilities	$100,000
Shareholder Equity	$8,000
Total Liabilities & Shareholder Equity	$108,000

To keep our mythical bank example simple let's assume that no depositor will withdraw their cash for the first year. Each of them is invested in a savings product with a one year restriction on withdrawal. That is, they are required to keep their money in their account for at least one year after depositing it.

After the first year of operations 3-6-3 Bank should expect to earn $5,000 in interest on its portfolio of loans ($100,000 in loans with a 5% interest rate). The bank would be entitled to receive the entire $5,000 so long as there are no defaults or bad loans which might require the bank to write off some or all of the problematic loans. Since this was the first year of operations the bank was extremely careful about who it loaned money to and thankfully there were no defaults.

Out of the $5,000 received in interest on the loans, the bank has to pay $1,000 in interest to its depositors. This leaves $4,000 in income with which to pay salaries, operating costs, Federal Deposit Insurance and other miscellaneous fees that are incurred in the operation of a bank. With only $4,000 and the desire to reinvest and build the business the bankers decide to forgo a salary and continue to work for free (hey, it's a mythical bank, remember?). The sweat equity and skills of the founders is valuable and they are fortunate to incur only $3,000 in operating expenses.

So to review, 3-6-3 Bank earned $5,000 in interest on its loans, paid out $1,000 in interest to depositors and incurred $3,000 in expenses. At this stage of the game they don't have any other income coming in. Most banks will actually earn what's referred to as non-interest income, which is simply income received in addition to that from "earning assets" (like loans or investment securities), such as from wealth management, data processing and so forth.

This leaves our fledgling operation with $1,000 in pre-tax profit. Since the bank is new and the lending appears to be solid, to keep things simple (for illustrative purposes), its decided that they don't need to reserve anything for future loan losses. The bank determines its tax rate on the $1,000 in operating income and after paying Uncle Sam $330 the bankers are left with a profit of $670 which they simply retain instead of reinvesting it in new loans or securities.

If we were to create a simple income statement for 3-6-3 Bank it would look like the following:

Interest income	$5,000
Interest expense	$1,000
Amount for loan losses	$0
Net interest income	$4,000
Non-Interest Income	$0
Operating expenses	$3,000
Pre-tax operating profit	$1,000
Taxes	$330
Net income	$670

For a brand new bank this isn't all that bad. In fact, it's actually pretty good! The five friends gather together and over burgers (what else?) review how they've done for their first year in business. 3-6-3 Bank earned a return on assets (ROA) of 0.62% ($670/$108,000) and a return on equity (ROE) of 8.3% ($670/$8,000). Given that the bank is in its first year of operation these are quite satisfactory results.

But all good things must end. One problem with our hypothetical bank is they don't have much cushion if one of their loans goes bad. If a borrower does not pay their loan on a timely basis the loan becomes past due. A bank will work hard to collect on past due loans as quickly as possible before the loan becomes even more distressed.

If the borrower does not pay their loan for a long enough time (typically 90 days, but this varies depending on the circumstances) it will eventually be moved from being a performing loan to a non-performing loan (NPL).

In banking parlance it's become a 'non-accrual loan' which is a loan that is no longer earning interest for the bank. When loans enter non-accrual status the bank shifts its focus from trying to collect interest to recovering the principal of the loan.

Soon after the end of the first year 3-6-3 Bank hits its first speed bump. One of its borrowers, named Elmo Mistakenly, with a $5,000 loan, has financial difficulties and payments start to arrive later and later before they stop altogether.

The bankers begin to worry that they potentially may need to write down the loan to Elmo. This simply means that they will change the 'value' of the loan on their books from the $5,000 it currently is to some lesser amount (which may be zero). This is what is known as a 'charge-off'.

Remember that after their first year of operations they chose to keep the entire $670 of net income in cash (retained earnings) instead of reinvesting it in new loans or other assets. In its most simplistic form, the bank has regulatory capital of $8,670 or 8.02%, which is slightly above the required minimum.

If the loan to Elmo Mistakenly defaults and they are required to write it down to zero, 3-6-3 Bank's capital will shrink to $3,670. If the bank's capital falls below the regulatory minimum their regulator will require them to raise additional capital through either an equity offering, preferred stock issuance or through a debt issuance. None of these results are ideal for existing shareholders.

Most banks have some level of non-performing assets (NPAs) at all times of operation. Any NPAs are troubling, but there are nuances to NPAs. A bank whose NPA trend is decreasing, for example, is generally viewed as better than one where the trend is increasing.

The NPA trend is important, but even more important is the rate of charge-offs (i.e. write downs). If a loan defaults and the bank is unable to recover all or some portion of the principal, the bank will need to charge-off that portion that is lost. Typically, a bank with NPAs of 2% (as measured against total asset value) might have a charge-off rate of 0.15% or less. This would indicate that the bank is able to recover a decent amount of value from the loans in non-accrual or default status.

Our five friends started 3-6-3 Bank because they thought it was a good way to make money, but also to be a part of and help the local community. They operate in a small town and know Elmo Mistakenly personally. Terms are worked out that are agreeable to both the bank and Elmo so that he can make a lower payment and the bank can avoid a total loss. This is what is known as a 'troubled debt restructuring' (TDR). It's better than a write off, but a significant amount of TDRs will find themselves in trouble again.

As you can probably see from our discussion of 3-6-3 Bank, the bankers are going to have a very long journey if they wish to expand utilizing only organic growth. If they wish to expand anytime before they're gumming their food, they will likely need to take on additional equity capital (via common stock or preferred shares) or borrow funds via a debt issuance or similar transaction. Debt counts towards regulatory capital, but not as much as equity or preferred stock. Any of these will enable them to have a larger capital base and, thus, enable more lending.

So there you have it. Now you know how a bank works, what it does and how it makes money. It isn't as complicated as you thought, is it? Well . . . .

In theory it's very easy to start a bank, gather deposits, start loaning out money and voilá, you're in business. The reality is much different. There are a number of regulatory hurdles and compliance issues we didn't touch on. Regulators are very strict about who can start a bank and have become even more strict in the wake of the financial crisis. There is also the work to set up back office operations, establish a branch, hire employees and so on.

Despite all of the hoops, speed bumps, hurdles and road blocks, it's easy to envision how one might start a bank, but wouldn't it be better to buy into an already functioning institution with established management? There are two paths to gaining ownership of a bank: one, begin the long process of starting one from scratch or, two, buy shares in an existing bank. It's far easier and preferable to buy into an existing institution and that's what the rest of this book will deal with - evaluating banks as investments.

4 ARE BANK STOCKS RISKY?

Are investments in bank stocks risky?

One of the authors had a very lively conversation recently with someone who claimed that banks are completely un-investable. This fellow's arguments were the same as most coming out of the financial crisis: banks are over-levered, their balance sheets are black boxes, they're too complex, they're loaded with derivatives, they would have gone under if not for accounting gimmicks keeping them alive, and so on and so forth. Had this person ever actually looked at a bank's financial statements? He hadn't, but that didn't get in the way of his very strong opinions. He's not alone. For many years we've heard the same arguments in different forms as justification for avoiding bank investments.

For some reason banks are the hobgoblins of investing. They're thought of as scary. It isn't uncommon for investors to simply state that their portfolio is and will always be a bank-free zone. One can envision these investors walking around wearing t-shirts with a picture on the front of a circle and the word "BANK" in it with a line running through it. Yes, they feel that strongly about it!

The issue to be explored is whether banks actually are risky investments. And, if so, are they any riskier than any

29

other investments? Are there ways to mitigate the risks?

Are cars risky? Is a lawnmower risky? The answer is "yes" and "no". A lawnmower can be extremely risky to operate if you don't know what you're doing. Cars are risky if the person behind the wheel doesn't know how to drive, if they're distracted or if they're impaired due to substances or grooving to too much Beyoncé. If you decide to mow a steep, wet hillside with bare feet you're taking on a lot of risk - the risk of grave injury or even death.

In our daily lives we accept that risks abound, but if handled properly risks can be mitigated to an acceptable degree. For example, cars are risky, but we wear seatbelts and minimize distractions, bad behavior and the music we listen to in order to compensate. Lawnmowers are risky, but we're careful when we use them. The common theme is that many things in life have risk when one doesn't know what they're doing, but risks can be managed with knowledge and experience. The same applies to investing in securities of banks.

Whether we realize it or not all businesses and investments have risk and banks are no exception. There is no such thing as a risk free business or investment. If someone tries to tell you otherwise please put on your track shoes and run the other way as fast as possible.

Out of the laundry list of risks related to bank investments the two that seem to get people the most hot and bothered are (1) the leverage of banks and (2) the balance sheet as a black box and the related complexity of banks. This chapter will discuss those risks. This isn't to give short shrift to the various other risks inherent in bank investing, but they are of somewhat secondary importance, at least in the minds of many investors.

LEVERAGE

To many people the biggest risk in the banking industry is leverage - banks are inherently levered entities. Leverage is simply the use of borrowed funds (which for a bank includes deposits), as opposed to equity, to purchase or otherwise acquire assets and run operations. In and of itself, leverage isn't good or bad, it's simply a tool. Leverage is a magnifier.

Think of a person buying a house for $100k with 20% down. The buyer pays $20k in cash to own a $100k asset. If the house appreciates 10% in price and is sold the buyer will realize a $10k, or 50%, gain on its investment. The house only appreciated 10%, but the buyer actually realized a 50% gain solely due to leverage.

The above example shows how leverage can magnify gains. However, leverage works both ways and it can also magnify losses. Take the same house example as above and assume that instead of 10% appreciation the housing market takes a dive (where have we seen this one before?) and the home is sold for $90k, or 10% less than the purchase price. In this situation the home is sold for only a $10k loss, but the homebuyer sees a 50% drop in the value of its investment ($90k - $80k mortgage = $10k equity value).

As we've discussed, at its most basic level a bank is an intermediary – a middle man, if you will - that helps connect people with money to those who need money. This is done via lending.

In performing the lending activity a bank ideally makes a small profit or spread (interest and fees), yet retains all of the risk that the principal of the loan won't be repaid.

Depositors, on the other hand, the ones whose money is being lent, bear essentially no risk due to government guarantees unless deposits are above a certain level. A bank is required to hold a small amount of capital against their loans, typically 8-10%, depending on a variety of factors.

Financial leverage is the concept that a business finances part of their operations with someone else's money. Much like the housing purchase example above, a bank only has a small slice of equity compared to their assets. But a bank is able to earn income on their entire asset base, not just the portion of the assets purchased with their equity.

If a bank has $1 in capital and a 10% capital ratio it means that $1 provides support for $10 in loans. Thus, this bank is levered 10 to 1. The beauty of leverage is that, as shown in the foregoing example, the bank earns interest on the full $10 in loans while only having $1 at risk. However, leverage cuts both ways. If things go wrong and just 10% of the value of the bank's assets go sour the bank could find itself in the bank equivalent of the airplane graveyard, FDIC receivership.

There is no question that leverage magnifies operational and other issues, but leverage isn't endemic to banks. The median aggregate leverage ratio for most industries is between 30-60%. To put this in equivalent banking terms, most companies have a 40-70% capital ratio. At first glance it would appear that banking is much riskier than virtually any other industry, save for companies with non-investment grade ratings and their median equivalent capital ratio of close to 8%.

There are two types of leverage implicit in a business: financial leverage and operating leverage. Financial leverage is discussed above. Operating leverage is the concept that a business incurs a certain amount of fixed costs to operate.

The best way to understand operating leverage is by looking at an example. Imagine you want to open a small shoe factory. It costs you $100 a month in rent and labor, and you had to spend $1,000 to buy the machine that makes the shoes. Materials for shoes cost $1 and each pair of shoes sells for $2. One hundred pairs of shoes must be sold each month to pay for rent, labor and materials (we will assume the $1,000 initial outlay on the machine was obtained with a loan from kind-hearted Aunt Linda). There is a tiny profit on the 101st pair of shoes sold. The $1 in profit starts to pay back the $1,000 from Aunt Linda for the shoe machine. Each additional pair of shoes sold above the 100th pair is increasingly profitable.

The above example demonstrates the idea of operational leverage. There is a fixed cost and once those costs are covered each additional unit sale increases profits. This is because the cost in terms of rent, labor and materials (at least at some base level) isn't dynamic, it's fixed. As we sell more and more shoes these fixed costs become smaller and smaller on a percentage basis as compared to revenues.

This type of leverage is beneficial for the business as long as unit sales increase, but can be very negative for a business when volume decreases. This is because the fixed costs are fixed in good times, but fixed in bad times as well. If the company can't sell enough units to cover fixed costs they'll incur a loss, which is problematic even if a business only has modest financial leverage. That is because the magnitude of the company's loss increases as unit volume decreases. Eventually a tipping point is reached where the company isn't selling enough units to cover costs, including debt payments, and the company is forced into bankruptcy.

When operational leverage and financial leverage are combined there are many companies that have similar leverage characteristics to banks. Yes, there are many companies with little to no debt and/or almost no operational leverage, but there are plenty that do have them. The issue isn't whether an institution is levered or not, but how the leverage is handled.

Banking can be thought of as a business of exclusion. Banks are more or less market takers on deposit and lending rates. That is, they generally must do what the market as a whole dictates as it relates to rates on loans and deposits. A bank might be able to make a few extra points at the margin, but deposit taking and lending are in most cases commodity businesses that are incredibly competitive. If the national average is a rate of 4.25% for a mortgage it's unlikely that a consumer will be able to find a bank willing to lend at 3.5% if they just search hard enough and ask nicely.

Because banks are taking deposits and making loans at the market rate the levers they have to control their performance are the types and quality of the loans they make and their expenses. When we say banking is a business of exclusion it's because bankers need to be able to walk away from questionable loans, whether as a result of the quality of the loan itself or the pricing. In an environment where people need money it is prudent to pass on most deals and only extend loans to the best borrowers at the best possible prices.

Interestingly, if a bank pays the average rate on deposits, earns the average rate on loans, avoids bad lending and has average expenses, they aren't an average bank, but an above-average bank.

BLACK BOXES AND COMPLEXITY

After leverage the second most popular reason for not investing in banks is because their balance sheets are "black boxes" and their structures are unnecessarily complex. We've illuminated how banks work and trust that a few layers of complexity have been removed. Hopefully, you no longer think of banks as the investments that go bump in the night!

However, a frequent claim is that banks are opaque and "black boxes". People aren't sure exactly what goes in and they sure as heck aren't sure what's coming out. Particularly after the financial crisis, a frequent charge leveled at banks was that no one knows what they do, what they own or what they're worth.

Here's a question: do you REALLY understand what's on any company's balance sheet? Is it possible that General Electric inadvertently overvalued some of their inventory amongst the $17b held on their balance sheet? Is it possible that the array of t-shirts and jeans at The Gap aren't the "true" valuations? How many companies out there are furnishing financials with wildly inflated property or asset values that managers with rose-colored glasses think might be obtainable someday, sometime? We're not even talking about fraud or misdirection. It's just that it isn't always possible to firm up a perfect valuation.

In actuality, banks are not as opaque as many industrial companies. Banks are required to file detailed financial reports with the FDIC on a quarterly basis. These reports describe banks at a very granular level, a level not found in SEC filings or elsewhere. Although, a caveat worth noting is that the FDIC's quarterly reports are written with the regulator in mind, not investors.

Investors might be comforted when reading the financial statements of an industrial knowing that inventory is hard goods, but one never knows what the condition of a company's inventory or plant and property truly is. Maybe the company overstated the value of their equipment, or maybe the equipment is decades old and hanging on by a thread. We don't know when management makes a sizable capital purchase if they went with the cheapest or the highest quality supplier.

In addition, while there are challenges in valuing any asset it is unclear why a portfolio of loans is deemed to be too difficult to value while an insurance company's book of business is not. Or, why a loan which has a ready market is just based on "mark to make believe" while a warehouse full of purple leggings is deemed able to be sold at any time.

Let's shrink the argument and consider a small industrial company like George Risk Industries for a second. They hold on a relative basis a lot of securities, a few million in cash and some fixed assets. They breakdown the securities in their annual report into very broad categories such as equities, municipal bonds and mutual funds. However, we don't know what funds they own or why they've lagged the market with their asset mix. We also don't know if their $4m in fixed assets are old machines held together with a bit of duct tape, prayer and a "git-r-done" attitude, or if their factory is full of top of the line equipment.

Contrast a situation like George Risk Industries with that of a bank that's not a megabank. Banks are required to provide financials detailing exactly what's on their balance sheet. From the types of loans they've made to the maturity schedule, it's possible to know on a quarterly basis things like what proportion of their loans are maturing in the next year. The same is true for deposit accounts. Investors can see that a bank has 27 accounts with between $100k-$250k or that it holds $48m in deposits for local governments. The amount of granular information banks provide is astounding (and outstanding too!).

It's not just the sheer volume of information that's important, although it is important. It's that this information is available for a bank's balance sheet and banks are somewhat unique in that they make their money almost solely from their balance sheet. An industrial company, as opposed to a financial company, takes a bunch of raw materials, smashes them together and produces a gizmo (or, perhaps, a widget when the mood strikes). The sales price of the gizmo/widget minus the cost of the materials and labor to build it is the company's gross profit. Companies are very private about this information and consider their input costs to be a trade secret. Investors see the financials, but have to guess as to the input costs necessary to generate the company's results.

Since banks make money primarily from their balance sheet investors have the ability to see all of the raw "input costs" that flow to the income statement. Ever wonder why two banks in the same city with the same lending area and deposit base have different degrees of profits? It's easy to determine why. After analyzing the expense profile, look at the types of loans each bank has made, as well as the related loan maturity schedule. Then examine the deposit situation for each bank and look at the types of accounts they have and the rates paid on each type of account. All of this information is public and easily accessible.

Generally, the "banks as black box" argument is valid only when discussing the largest financials, including in some cases large regional banks, but more specifically when one is referring to megabanks, i.e. the four horsemen: JP Morgan, Bank of America, Citigroup and Wells Fargo. Together, these banks hold approximately $10.26T in assets out of the approximate $26.4T in aggregate banking assets as of the end of Q2 2017. That means that 38.87% of all banking assets in the US are held by the top four banks, while the other 5,796 banks hold the remaining 61% of US banking assets. That is quite a wide divergence.

There is probably no one who knows exactly what these four behemoths are doing. They have exceptionally large and complicated balance sheets with a lot of moving parts. Are all or any of them hiding risk on their balance sheets? It's very likely due to the sheer size of the organizations and their complexity. The issue is one of magnitude. In 2012, a rogue trader (nicknamed by the media as the "London Whale") at JP Morgan caused a loss of $6.2b. JP Morgan was able to absorb this loss and move forward without an impact to their business. Consider that of the 5,796 banks in existence in the US at the end of Q2 2017 only 274 had more than $6b in total assets. The London Whale made three bad trades that in the aggregate lost more money than 97% of the banks in the US hold in assets on their balance sheets.

The London Whale story is emphasized to show the magnitude of divergence between the four megabanks and the rest of the banking industry. They are likely hiding risk that even they don't know about and their utter massiveness has become a liability to the US economy.

The FDIC published a working paper in 2015

investigating how the housing crisis might have impacted the US economy differently had our banking system in 2008 been as diversified as it was in 1992. The paper showed that if our banking system had been less concentrated the impact of the housing crisis would have been 40% lower than what we experienced. Our indifference to concentration has created an economic liability and a huge risk. The four largest banks have become so important to the US economy, and their impact so exaggerated, that they are considered too big to fail and are implicitly now backstopped by the US government. The government doesn't seem to have the stomach to sit by and watch any of these institutions fail and because of that an element of moral hazard has been introduced into the system.

The biggest actual risk to a bank is the same risk that exists for any company - operational risk. This is the risk that management makes bad decisions. Perhaps they grow too quickly or in the wrong direction, hire the wrong people, make bad loans or other investments and so on. All businesses have operational risks. All human beings are flawed and by definition a business is an entity run for and by human beings (at least for now until AI take over).

The primary operational risk related to a bank is the risk of making bad loans. There are various factors that can result in bad lending, such as poor quality borrowers and growing too fast (with loosening standards) to simply operating in an area without good economics.

Banks do not share in the upside with their borrowers. If a borrower obtains a $90k loan to pay for a $100k house and then later the borrower sells the house for $200k, the bank will still only receive a return of its $90k plus interest. They don't earn more if the house appreciates or if a business they've lent money to has a record breaking year.

The opposite of this is also true. If a home falls in value the homeowner may still owe the same amount but if they can't pay it in many areas there is no recourse to the borrower, only the property. In a nutshell, lending can be described as having limited upside with lots of downside. At best you get what you expected or hoped for. At worst you get that door on the show "Let's Make a Deal" with the big jar of pickles (just kidding, you actually get nothing, not even a jar of pickles to enjoy and share with friends and family).

In the world of banking risk reduction means avoiding bad loans. This is easier said than done. Banks feel pressure from their shareholders and from their board to continually grow. If the pressure is strong enough on the lending and underwriting team it won't be long until some poor quality loans slip through the cracks. Bad lending is almost never uncovered immediately. It takes time for borrowers to run into problems or a group of loans to a specific industry to fall apart. Borrowers borrow with the best of intentions. No one except an outright criminal takes out a loan without the expectation that they'll be able to pay it back.

The best way for investors to assess risk in bank securities is to look at a bank's past lending history. How has the bank performed when the region or industries they operate in experienced a recession or downturn? How has the bank dealt with the bankruptcy of a major borrower? These are the types of issues that one can examine in order to get a sense for what the bank is made of.

Investors often use the phrase "the trend is your friend" to explain the strong force that inertia can play in investments. A similar thought can be applied to banking. A bank's portfolio decays over a period of time in the same way that it improves over a period of time. If a bank experiences a seemingly sudden deterioration of their portfolio it's probably time to reconsider the investment. Likewise, a bank that's experiencing increasing credit issues should be deemed riskier than one that has slightly elevated metrics but is stable.

Consider two identical banks, Bank A and Bank B. The following two tables show their NPLs as a percentage of total loans.

	Q1	Q2	Q3	Q4
Bank A	2.70%	2.68%	2.71%	2.73%

	Q1	Q2	Q3	Q4
Bank B	1.70%	1.84%	1.88%	2.5%

If one were looking at the absolute level of NPLs then Bank B would be considered a safer bank. Yet, all things being equal it's not the absolute level that matters as much as the trend. Bank A's NPLs are stable. There are slight fluctuations from quarter to quarter, but this is because a bank's loan portfolio naturally fluctuates with payoffs and loan originations.

The bank with the more worrying trend is Bank B. They started with a lower level of NPLs, but this number has been steadily increasing and spiked somewhat in Q4. In a situation like this the investor needs to consider or reconsider the risk associated with the investment.

The answer to the question "are banks risky?" is yes, but so are all businesses, as well as virtually everything we do in life. The question isn't whether risk exists, but the type and magnitude of risk that's of concern. There is a risk that a house will collapse at any time, but the chance of it happening is so small that it's not worth worrying about. The same can be said for many banking risks as well.

One thing that makes banks different from traditional companies from a leverage standpoint is that banks are experts in managing risk. This is what they do (or are supposed to do anyway) all day long. For an industrial company borrowing to finance equipment the sky is the limit when it comes to the potential return on their investment. Banks, however, lend money with known return characteristics.

A bank's risk department is responsible for ensuring that the bank doesn't concentrate too many loans in a given sector. The underwriting department's mandate is to attempt to write loans that will not lose value. Banks aspire to perfect underwriting records even though that's impossible. In addition, a bank can manage their deposit cost to better match up with their lending portfolio risk.

5 INVESTING IN BANKS

If you recall in Chapter 2, we discussed how one advantage to investing in banks is that it is an investment in a cross section of the economy (remember Bob & Son's Plumbing?). An investment in a community bank is an investment in a local economy, an investment in a regional bank is an investment in a regional economy, while an investment in a megabank is an investment in the economy of the good ol' United States in general (and beyond).

To recap, only a very small number of businesses in the United States are publicly listed. The vast majority of businesses that provide jobs and support local and regional economies are privately held. An investor never really has the opportunity to invest directly into any of these private businesses. What an investor does have is the ability to invest in a bank that does business with dozens, hundreds or even thousands of local private companies. Banks make loans and take deposits from local businesses.

In fact, some investors prefer to use banks as a surrogate to take advantage of a locally booming economy. For example, there is a fund that invests primarily in small banks in Western Pennsylvania, Eastern Ohio and West Virginia due to the fact that these banks have tremendous exposure to the Marcellus Shale Region and the related energy concerns. The fund's premise was these local banks would outperform as they benefitted from the oil and gas boom. But alas, all good things must come to an end and the oil and gas boom is no exception. The fund's investors received an outsized ride on the way up, and on the way down as well.

There is an undeniable learning curve to understanding banking. The good news is that suffering through the process has benefits. All banks file financials in virtually the exact same manner and their businesses are all generally the same: take deposits, loan money, and earn the spread. There are nuances across various banks, of course, but in general a bank with $800m in assets in North Dakota can be directly compared to a bank with $800m in assets in New Jersey.

The ability to compare companies across geographies in such a manner is unique to banking. Non-bank companies come in all different shapes and sizes and even close competitors may have dramatic differences. In most industries there are at most a handful of listed companies. An investor analyzing two or more companies in the same industry will learn general traits of the industry that aren't easily transferable to other industries. Knowing about mine production efficiency doesn't help when analyzing a health care company.

Banks begin to differ when they add products and services around their core banking business, such as financial advisory, trust management and private banking, all of which can entail highly customized products or services. But once the core business of a bank is understood, these "extras" can be easily slotted into the analysis.

While banking is generally a commodity business, paradoxically, it's also a niche business. The cost to a consumer or business of switching banks is very high. Opening a new bank account is slow due to regulations and all of the required paperwork. Beyond the initial inconvenience and time commitment required to open a new account, customers incur more time and hassle when they switch their electronic bill payment and direct deposit to their new account. Completing any of these tasks might not be complicated or difficult, but to a consumer the tasks in the aggregate may seem overwhelming for not that much of an advantage or benefit. For many customers a bank is simply good enough. It provides enough of what they need and isn't bad enough for them to go through the pain of switching.

So here we are. You've bought the argument that you should at least consider adding banks to your investment portfolio. But now the questions are piling up. What is the meaning of life and love? How do we achieve world peace? Can a bionic man still be made for $6m? And, how do you value banks?

We will get to all of that, but to start here is a brief summary of some different valuation techniques.

Relative Valuation

Sometimes the best measure of value is relative value. That is, what is the value of a company as compared to competitors in the same or a similar line of business. When potential homeowners are looking to buy a house they will compare the house (and the asking price) they like with other similar houses to determine if the value of their potential new home is fair. The problem with this type of valuation for most businesses is that it's often difficult to find enough comparison candidates with available information in order to make a relative valuation. Fortunately, this is not the case with banks. Due to the transparency enforced by the FDIC, banks are required to submit financial reports quarterly that are in the same identical format making a comparison much easier.

Banks can be compared to each other, or groups of other banks, based on their operating metrics. They can also be compared against a bank stock index to determine the relative value compared to other banks.

There are a number of different bank stock indexes ranging from the well known KBW Bank Index to the Dow Jones Bank Index all the way down to the NASDAQ Community Bank Index.

An index is simply a grouping of a certain set of stocks based on one or more specific criteria. An index allows the tracking of performance of that group of stocks typically based on averages, but in some cases based on different computations. Bank stock indexes thus represent price movements for bank stocks (or certain bank stocks) in general.

It is this representation that makes the valuation metrics for a bank stock index valuable. If the price to book (P/B) multiple of a bank stock index is 1.2 that indicates that on average representative bank stocks trade at a 20% premium to their book value (shareholders' equity). There are of course some bank stocks with higher multiples and some with lower multiples, but the index is representative of a certain set of bank stocks as a whole. Thus, finding a bank stock with a substantially lower multiple as compared to that of the index is an indication of a potentially undervalued situation.

It should be noted that comparing a bank's valuation metrics to those of an index is merely a starting point for finding a bank investment.

FIXED VALUATION

Given a specific set of bank stocks there will always be some that trade for multiples below the average and some that trade above the average. After all, this blend is what makes an average to begin with.

Another way to value bank stocks besides the relative valuation approach is to use fixed valuation tools. This could include valuing a bank stock based on its potential acquisition value or its discounted cash flows. Both approaches will be discussed below.

ACQUISITION VALUATION

It would be foolish to assume that every bank is operating at their maximum potential. The reality is that some are, but many aren't. There are a variety of reasons that a bank might be under performing; maybe it's intentional, or maybe management just doesn't know how to maximize the resources they have. Regardless, if a bank isn't living up to their potential then there is room for improvement.

Improvements at banks usually come in the same form. A bank is purchased and the new management implements procedures and products that reduce expenses and increase profitability. A bank that is acquired and operating under different management with a different expense structure could be dramatically more profitable than it is currently.

An acquisition valuation attempts to estimate what costs could be saved at a bank if it were to be acquired. In the case of a bank with excess capital an acquisition valuation would also look at potential earnings from putting the bank's excess capital to work.

One advantage for investors using an acquisition valuation is that this method is the same method bankers use to view potential acquisition targets. An investor who builds out acquisition valuations looks to purchase banks for a discount to their acquisition value.

DISCOUNTED CASH FLOW VALUATION

Traditional investment theory states that a business is only worth the cash it can generate. This theory attempts to project all of the future earnings for a business and then discount those earnings back to calculate a present value. This is called a discounted cash flow analysis.

A discounted cash flow approach is common when considering non-bank investments, but it can also be applied to banks. Since banks are regulated entities they can't use 100% of their cash flow to pay dividends and buyback shares. Their regulators put limits on what needs to be retained and what can be returned to shareholders.

The adapted discounted cash flow approach for banks is to substitute dividends for cash flow. An investor would projects potential future dividend payments into eternity and then discount those back to calculate a present value.

While a discounted cash flow approach is sound it isn't common when evaluating banks. However, bank investors should at least be aware of how it works.

SUMMARY

The approach an investor uses to value a bank stock is dependent on their overall investment framework. Investors who prefer to trade stocks might be more interested in relative valuation, whereas investors who are longer term oriented are more likely to use a fixed valuation, acquisition valuation or discounted cash flow approach.

There is no 'best' way to value banks, rather there are different tools that can be used at different times depending on your goals as an investor.

6 BANK INVESTING APPROACHES

There are as many approaches to investing as there are investors. Most of these approaches result in some form of successful outcome, otherwise they would be discontinued as quickly at they were created. Some investors focus on trading around news, others buy and hold for the long term. Some like to purchase beat up companies hoping for a turnaround, and others prefer to purchase fast growers.

The goal of this chapter is to highlight the most common approaches to investing in banks. These are not the only ways to invest. Maybe you'll come up with something on your own. One author met an investor who prefers to invest only in Iowa banks, while another investor prefers Pennsylvania and Kansas banks because he has relatives in those states. Regardless of your individual approach there is value in understanding how other people in the market invest. After all, you will likely be buying or selling to someone using one of these strategies. You might be able to gain a slight edge by understanding not only your own strategy, but your counterparty's strategy as well.

VALUE APPROACH

We start with the value approach because your authors are biased, this is the approach that both of us prefer and use. But don't let our excitement sway you from evaluating other approaches. We are open minded investors. Whatever works for you is good with us!

Value investing was first popularized by Benjamin Graham (along with David Dodd) in the 1930s with his seminal book, "Security Analysis". Graham posited that investors should try to buy $1.00 worth of value for $0.50 and should buy stocks like they purchase groceries rather than perfume.

Within a bank investing context this often means purchasing banks that are trading at low multiples, such as P/B, Price to Tangible Book Value (P/TBV), or P/E.

Value investing can be rewarding because it gives investors a solid, repeatable framework to invest within. Purchase banks at a discount to book value and sell when they reach book value (or a small premium to book value), rinse, repeat, and retire in the Caribbean.

A potential downfall for this type of approach is that many times banks sell at discounts to book value or low P/E multiples for valid reasons. As an example a bank might be struggling with a non-performing loan portfolio and the bank's depressed trading multiple reflects a potential loan book charge-off (i.e. write-down). In this scenario the bank's discount to book value is warranted because of the impending charge-offs.

The value approach works because humans are emotional beings. It's very difficult to ignore your feelings and invest in a bank with a depressed share price when there is bad news swirling around the investment.

A value investor is able to harness their emotions. They can invest in something cheap when market sentiment is negative and then sell their positions when they become fairly valued, which usually coincides with positive market sentiment. Some say value investors are born with a gene that attracts them to cheap stocks. It's the same gene that leads people to shop the clearance racks and rummage through the discount bins. If you've ever found yourself thinking that "sale" items are too expensive compared to what's on clearance then value investing might be for you.

RELATIVE APPROACH

Have you ever heard the joke where someone asks "how do you outrun a bear?" The punchline to the joke is "you don't outrun a bear, you outrun everyone else and let the bear get them." The relative value approach is similar in that there are no absolutes. It's not the metric a bank trades at that's important, but how the bank compares to peer banks.

Before the Great Recession it wasn't uncommon for a bank to trade for 2x or 3x book value or more. Then, in the midst of the Great Recession, investors wouldn't touch banks at even 1x book value, sometimes 65% or 75% of book value was considered too rich. And now, years later, many of the same banks are again trading at 1.5x or 2x book value.

One way to invest in a valuation cycle like this is to hold cash and buy at the bottom, then sell on the way up. But this approach can leave an investor holding cash for years waiting for just the right time to buy. It's hard to time the market.

A better way to invest in the broader valuation cycles is to buy banks trading at a discount to peers and sell when the valuation gap closes.

Regardless of where the market is in a given cycle, bank valuations tend to cluster. If a bank is undifferentiated in their business they will trade near their peers absent unusual circumstances. Outlier banks, those that trade at steep discounts or premiums to peers, can often be traced to a specific cause. A cause being some piece of news, or peculiar item, about a specific bank that investors either prize or despise.

An example of this might be a bank with a lower than average efficiency ratio that generates higher returns on equity. In a given market cycle investors might value low efficiency and high returns on equity and trade the bank's shares at a premium to peers.

Another example is when a bank has an all-star management team. Investors get excited over exceptional managers and their potential for a company even if those expectations don't always fall to the bottom line. Banks with storied management teams, or management teams that are winning "Banker of the Year" awards, tend to trade at a premium to peers.

Likewise, when a bank is regarded as out of touch, old fashioned, or located in a dying area shares will trade at a discount to peers. You don't find too many investors bragging that The First Bank of Nowhere with its rural presence and disdain for online banking is a screaming buy, even if it is trading for 50% of tangible book value. Investors are inclined to brag about growth, regardless of whether that growth leads to investment value.

The way an investor can utilize a relative valuation approach is to find banks that are out of sync with peers. We can define under and over-valued as the following:

Undervalued bank – A bank that trades at a discount to other banks with similar characteristics.

Overvalued bank – A bank that trades at a premium to other banks with similar characteristics.

Banks should trade in line with peers if they are similar to peers. This makes intuitive sense - goods that are the same are priced the same, whereas goods with different characteristics are priced differently. Banks with similar business models, similar customer bases, in similar locales should trade at similar valuations. This is the efficient market at work.

When a bank doesn't trade in line with similar peers it's the job of the investor to investigate why. Maybe the market is wrong in which case the investor is presented with a money making opportunity. But, maybe the market is right and the discount or premium to peers is warranted.

Bank investors who use a relative investing approach make money when they can correctly ascertain why discounts and premiums to peers exist and then take action by buying or selling and waiting for those valuation gaps to close.

To use the relative investing approach one needs to be skeptical, curious and approach their research like a detective aiming to solve a mystery. Most importantly the investor needs to be able to act based on their own research and facts regardless of what the market is saying or seems to be saying.

FOLLOWING ACTIVISTS AND INSIDERS

There is an allure to riding the coattails on an investment with someone smarter or more informed than you. In theory, bank insiders know their bank from top to bottom and are intimately familiar with the most minute details of the company. The idea is that when bank insiders purchase stock in their own bank they are making a statement. A statement that they believe the bank's shares to be cheap and that they are putting their money where their mouth is.

Insider buying isn't the slam dunk that some investors would make it out to be. Even though an insider purchasing shares in their own company is a vote of confidence, it doesn't always mean as much for outside investors.

Bank managers often aren't objective when they purchase shares in their own bank. They are biased towards their own institution as it provides them with an income and, for some people, mental benefits as well. An investor should also keep in mind that the insider likely didn't evaluate other potential bank investment opportunities and decide that their bank was more attractively valued than such other options before purchasing shares.

In general, bank insiders purchase shares because they believe they're cheap. But what is cheap to a banker might not be cheap to an investor.

Just like insider buying isn't a reliable indicator of value, insider selling isn't either. Insiders sell shares for a variety of reasons. They might need money to buy a new car or house, to pay country club dues, to pay for a vacation or fund their children's education.

A somewhat related, but different approach, is investing in banks where activist bank investors are involved.

Whereas management doesn't objectively evaluate all opportunities and pick the best investment, a bank activist investor ostensibly does. The bank activist investor's mandate is to earn a market beating return for their investors. They do this by evaluating banks and investing in the ones that they think will be open (or susceptible) to activist overtures and will give them the best return.

Bank management can be a cushy job full of perks and outside investors see that as an opportunity for cost reductions. The typical playbook for an activist investor is as follows. The activist will buy up to 9.9% of the target bank. The reason for the 9.9% threshold is that the FDIC considers an investor who owns more than 10% of a bank to be a controlling shareholder and subject to regulations regarding when they can buy shares and what they can do with them. In an effort to avoid being regulated bank activists limit their ownership stakes to 9.9% or less of a target bank.

Once an activist owns a significant portion of the bank they contact management in an effort to strongly encourage them to change their entrenched ways. Sometimes the threat of an activist take-over is enough for bankers to change, although it's rare they change on their own without some prodding. Usually an activist needs to get personally involved, either through a proxy battle or by exerting steady and constant pressure (public and private) on management to undertake value creating actions.

It might seem strange that an investor who owns no more than 9.9% of a given bank can have an outsized impact. But, there are a few things working in the favor of activist bank investors. The first is that bank executives rarely own more than 9.9% of the bank stock themselves. Typically, in fact, the activist is the largest single shareholder. This means that even though management controls the inner workings of the bank they are outvoted in the Board room.

The second factor that makes following activists attractive is that activists are always involved in underperforming banks. There is no reason for activist investors to get involved in a bank which is outperforming peers, growing and creating shareholder value. Activists work in situations where management has destroyed shareholder value for years, where banks are stagnant or shrinking, and the shareholder base is weary. Most shareholders look at activists as saviors. Many of these investors would like to initiate the type of change that activists propose, but individual shareholders don't have enough clout on their own. This means that when an activist starts a proxy battle they are likely to garner votes in excess of their direct holdings. Shareholders who are fed up with management will side with an activist in the hope that something will change at the institution.

The outcome for most activist situations is that an underperforming bank is forced into a sale or merger with a bank performing satisfactorily. It's very hard to change entrenched culture and a lot easier to sell an institution to a competitor down the street, across the state, or across the country. While activists would probably love to change the culture of some of their holdings, it's easier to convince the Board to sell and move onto the next investment target.

Growth Approach

There is a saying that "if you aren't growing, you're dying." That about sums up the situation for many investors who feel that where there is no growth there is no reason to invest.

Buying growing banks is probably the simplest approach to bank investing. At the 10,000 foot level one can look for a bank growing their business at a rate faster than peers, buy its stock, and watch the investment blossom as the market rewards the bank for its growth.

It would seem that investing for growth is simple, but as one dives into the details it becomes apparent there are important nuances. Let's first discuss growth approaches in general before exploring potential growth pitfalls.

The most common approach is to look for banks with growing assets. Assets are the engine that drive all aspects of profitability at a bank. A low amount of assets limits the profits a bank can make, while more assets allow for greater profitability and give a bank flexibility. A bank endowed with assets doesn't have to reach for yield to earn money and can be choosier as to who they lend money to.

There is a natural level of asset depletion resulting from borrowers paying down theirs loans over time. This happens because after a loan is originated it's principal is typically paid down over the period or term of the loan (unless such loan has a balloon payment due). This leaves the bank with a situation where loans continuously need to be originated, otherwise their loan book would gently glide towards zero as borrowers pay off their obligations.

For a bank to grow they need to originate an amount of loans in excess of the natural payoff rate for their loan portfolio. In other words, a bank is like a person in a pool. If they do nothing they sink. With a minimal level of exertion treading water a person will float, but won't move. And with even more exertion a person will be propelled forward.

Banks are in the business of loaning money. If they

stop or slow down the bank starts to shrink.

Assets can be grown through acquisition or organically. Most bankers would prefer to grow their assets organically, but it isn't always feasible. The various marketplaces for loans (absent a niche or some other distinguishing feature) is extremely competitive and without an above average lending team it's hard to find growth without compromising asset quality.

Growing through acquisitions is a perfectly reasonable strategy, and in most cases that's the typical route for a bank to grow.

There are two ways an investor can take advantage of a bank growing through acquisitions, either buy the bank building an empire, or purchase banks that are likely takeover candidates. Both approaches have pros and cons, and one isn't necessarily better than the other.

However, even though banks need to grow, not all growth is good growth. Sometimes in their quest for growth a bank can overextend themselves and end up in an unfavorable situation.

There are two specific pitfalls that might trip up a bank growing for the sake of growing. The first issue with growth is when lending standards are loosened in a desire make more loans and to grow faster. In the quest for a larger asset base, and in turn expanded profitability, a bank might ease up on who they consider extending a loan to. There is only so much credit demand in a given area, and if a bank attempts to grow faster than organic demand they either need to steal market share from other banks, or lower their standards and extend credit to borrowers who they wouldn't normally extend credit to.

When a bank is growing rapidly it's not uncommon for bad loans to slip into their portfolio. This could be because in the rush to close business proper due diligence isn't exercised, because a loan officer is junior and inexperienced, or a host of other factors. Often, it's not a single factor that leads to bad loans, but rather a confluence of factors.

When a bank is lending in a hot market and benefiting from the market's growth, investors need to be on the lookout for bad loans as well. Hot markets attract optimistic business plans that don't always withstand a moderate or poor economic environment. Some business plans only make sense in the midst of a hot market.

The second type of issue with growth is when a bank lowers their deposit quality standards. A bank's deposit base is their largest and cheapest funding source. Most banks grow deposits slowly and at a measured pace. An area with a population boom might be one of the only exceptions to this. Deposits tend to grow at a rate similar to the GDP growth rate plus inflation.

Banks need the support of deposits to grow their assets. If a bank is in a hurry to grow their assets they can bring in additional deposits either by offering unusually high rates on deposits or by using a broker network.

Deposits in whatever form support assets, but it's the deposit mix which affects a bank's profitability. This is discussed in detail in Chapter 10 A bank needs to find the balance between additional deposits and the cost for those additional deposits.

The worst deposit customers are the ones who are extremely rate sensitive. These are customers who move their money across the street when they can earn 0.10%

more on their savings. A bank can quickly attract deposits by offering to pay slightly more than rivals on savings products. This trick motivates the rate sensitive depositor population to move their money. The problem is if another bank offers a better rate these new deposits will walk out the door as fast as they walked in. Increasing savings product rates to attract deposits isn't a sustainable strategy as it becomes a race to the bottom.

Another source of funding is brokered deposits. Brokered deposits are deposits funded with certificates of deposit (CD) obtained through a brokerage network. Brokers like to offer a variety of financial instruments to their clients. Banks sell their CDs into these networks. The advantage for a bank is a brokerage network has a larger reach, and banks can fill funding holes quickly through brokered CDs.

The downside is brokered CDs are considered 'hot money'. Brokerage customers are savvy and are rate sensitive shoppers. They will move their money to the highest yielding CD once their current CD matures or if there is no early withdrawal penalty. This means a bank might fill their funding need for the short term, but once their brokered CD's mature the bank needs to compete on yield again in the marketplace. The more the bank pays for easy money the lower their profits.

There are a number of growth pitfalls to watch out for, but if such pitfalls are mitigated buying growing banks can be a profitable and sustainable strategy.

OTHER APPROACHES

We've covered the most popular ways to invest in bank stocks, but they aren't the only approaches investors use. The following are other bank investing approaches that are often a subset of one of the more popular approaches that has been discussed. These are covered in a summary fashion below.

Niche Banking Approach

There is a saying "In niches there are riches", which can be applied to banking or lending as easily as anything else.

In the banking industry there are a small number of lenders who lend to a very narrow set of customers. An example of this is a bank that focuses on auto lending, credit card lending, or specialized construction financing. An extreme example of this is the Farm Credit System, an almost parallel banking system that provides financing exclusively to farmers and agricultural businesses.

The Farm Credit System is a great example of a niche lender in that they're business model is focused entirely on one commercial group. But, they're a great example for another reason. Farm Credit Banks are mutual institutions; they're owned by their borrowers and unless you're a farmer or rancher it's impossible to become a shareholder. This is true for most niche lenders, the banks are privately held and effectively off limits to investors.

Niche lenders usually generate higher returns on capital and keep a tighter hold on risk. If you come across a traded niche lender they are worth further research.

Market Leader Approach

A subset of the growth approach is to buy market leaders. These are banks that are the stalwart in a given market and dominate lending and deposit market share. This strategy could even be simplified to buying nothing but the largest banks.

The market leader approach gives an investor a proxy investment into a sizable segment of the economy.

Dividend Approach

A very popular investment approach is to buy stocks for their dividends. Investors utilizing this approach are looking for current yield. They want a cash return on their investments now, not at some unspecified point in the future.

Banks can be great stocks for dividend investors. Most banks pay dividends, and some can have sizable yields. Besides deposit funding, banks fund their business with preferred stock, debt, and at times other esoteric financial instruments.

Bank equity is usually the lowest yielding security, but also the most readily liquid and available. If an investor is willing to forgo future appreciation for a higher current yield preferred stock or subordinated debt could fit the bill.

The danger for dividend investors is a bank's ability to pay dividends is governed by their regulator. In a financial crisis a regulator might demand a bank rebuild capital versus paying dividends to investors. This impacts investors who thought they'd purchased a guaranteed annuity stream of dividends. When a bank cuts their dividend it's accompanied by a share price decline in most cases. This is a double whammy for investors as their dividend goes missing and if they decide to sell they're forced to sell at a loss, or hold the stock without a dividend.

SUMMARY

As you can see there are a number of different ways to approach bank investing. The method you use will be based on your personality, your risk tolerance, and your worldview. There are some investors who are always looking for a bargain and will buy anything given a good enough price. Whereas other investors can't stomach the idea of owning a lower quality bank, even if the price more than compensates for this fact. You need to decide what method is best for you, and once that's been decided you'll then be in a position to know what valuation tools work best for your approach.

7 STRUCTURES/ENTITIES

When investors first start to look at banks there are two aspects that are often initially confusing. First, how the bank business model works and, second, the odd corporate structures banks sometimes employ.

At the most basic level (or, in the beginning, if you will) there are financial institutions referred to as "banks." These are entities that hold banking charters from the FDIC, are highly regulated and engaged in the business of banking.

In days of yore each bank was required to have a single bank charter, which meant each bank could have only one branch. Banks were not allowed to have multiple branches. This is the root cause of the reason that the United States is littered with so many banks, with a number of them in small towns serving small populations or other niche areas. In many cases, these banks are in the same building, in the same city and serving the same general clientele they have since before they were allowed to create branches.

The first regulation to loosen up the system was one that allowed banks to have multiple branches within the same state. For smaller banks, or banks content to serve a specific niche or market, this might have been fine. But other banks weren't content with this policy and wanted to grow beyond the boundaries of their state of formation.

The prohibition on crossing state lines was due in part to banks being regulated by the state banking regulators located in their state of formation. If a bank spanned two states there was the question of who would regulate them.

In the 1950s some banks devised a clever construct to get around the geographic limitation on bank branches. A bank was not allowed to have branches in more than one state, but what if there was a separate holding company that owned banks located in different states? A holding company, for example, could own a bank that's only in Connecticut and also own a bank that's only in New York. At the same time, and to make things even more convoluted, some of these holding companies were engaging in non-banking business. Banks were being included in corporate conglomerates and regulators didn't know how to handle it.

The Federal regulators (not to mention the various state regulators who had their toes being stepped on) didn't look too kindly on this circumvention and in 1956 passed the Bank Holding Company Act. The Act stipulated that bank holding companies would be regulated by the Federal Reserve and that banks would be banned from acquiring other banks except in the state they were headquartered in. The law also prohibited bank holding companies from engaging in non-financial business and owning securities of other financial institutions.

Although it was chipped away over the years, banks and bank holding companies operated in this geographic and business restrictive environment until 1994 when Congress passed the Riegle-Neal Interstate Banking and Branching Efficiency Act of 1994 (IBBEA). The IBBEA opened the door for federally chartered banks to branch and merge beyond their state borders and leveled the regulatory playing field. Banks were allowed to merge so long as they complied with applicable guidelines, including that both banks were "adequately capitalized and managed banks, subject to concentration limits, state laws and Community Reinvestment Act (CRA) evaluations."

Further restrictions on banks, such as owning non-financial companies, were removed in 1999 by the Gramm-Leach-Bliley Act. Although there had been some limited exceptions before, this opened the door for bank holding companies to own brokerages and other financial institutions.

Banking history is long and storied, but since we're not writing a sleep aid (and it's beyond the scope of this book anyway) we'll leave the further digging to you. There are numerous books written about the history of banking covered in dust in basements at libraries the world over. For those determined souls who possess the key ingredient of lots of coffee it's worth the time dusting off these tomes to find the nuggets of wisdom buried there. But for the rest of us, we move on.

The progression of banking over the years has led to a number of unusual corporate structures employed. Investors can take advantage of some of these structures. Regardless of how actionable any one structure is, it's worth discussing the most popular ones.

BANK HOLDING COMPANIES

The majority of banks utilize the holding company bank structure that was discussed briefly earlier in this chapter. The way this works is a corporation is created that owns all of the shares of the subsidiary bank(s), as well as any other businesses. For publicly traded bank holding companies, it's the top level (the holding company) that sells its stock to the public in an IPO.

Bank holding companies serve multiple purposes. The biggest advantage for a bank to employ a holding company structure is that there are fewer regulations on raising capital and the payment of dividends. As highly regulated entities banks require regulatory approval before paying dividends to shareholders since these dividends permanently reduce the bank's equity base. Essentially, the bank holding company structure provides more flexibility in this regard.

Prior to the Great Recession a popular method used to raise capital was to issue bank trust preferred securities (known as "TruPS"). Although bank regulators never permitted banks to issue TruPS, the Federal Reserve, on the other hand, which regulated bank holding companies never had an issue with them. TruPS were a cheap way for bank holding companies to raise capital. A bank holding company would issue TruPS and then downstream (i.e. send; note that money provided by a parent to a subsidiary is referred to as being "downstreamed", while funds that go from a subsidiary to a parent are referred to as being "upstreamed") the raised funds to their subsidiary bank(s), thus giving those subsidiary banks a higher capital ratio.

The bank holding company structure isn't all tea and cucumber sandwiches, however, and it can be problematic when the economy encounters a downturn.

Consider a scenario where a bank holding company issues debt, TruPS or another type of security in order to raise capital which they then downstream to their bank subsidiary. Although the holding company no longer has the money that was raised, it is on the hook for periodic interest payments, as well as the ultimate repayment of principal. These payments are funded almost entirely, if not fully, by dividends upstreamed by the bank subsidiary. If the economy hits a rough patch and the bank runs into trouble, they might not have the ability to pay dividends to their parent holding company. If the holding company can't pay interest on their outstanding interest bearing securities they'll end up in default, even though it's possible the subsidiary bank is ultimately viable and sound.

When analyzing the public securities of a bank holding company for a potential investment, one needs to examine both the holding company's financial statements as well as those of any subsidiary banks. A profitable and well capitalized bank might be owned by a holding company saddled with expensive debt or preferred securities (although, ironically, the reason the subsidiary bank might be well capitalized is because of that expensive debt or preferred securities!).

Likewise, a bank might be owned by a holding company with a clean balance sheet with considerable cash and assets. These assets will never appear on a bank's balance sheet as the bank and holding company are separate legal entities (although when looking at the financial statements of a bank holding company they are consolidated with their subsidiary bank the vast majority of the time).

MUTUAL BANKS

Mutual banks (or mutuals) are a subset of banking with their own experts, websites and even own culture. Hey, there are people who collect back scratchers, moist towelettes and even popcorn art, so why not people dedicated to a certain subculture of banking?

A mutual bank is a banking organization where the depositors are the owners of the bank, similar to a co-op. In most cases, these depositors don't even know that they own the bank, but legally they do. Mutuals were originally formed by like-minded groups who pooled funds as a way to offer low cost loans to members. Mutual banks are not all that different from credit unions.

The mutual bank structure was very popular in the U.S. in the 1800s and 1900s, but the problem for mutual institutions is there is no end game. A mutual bank has three choices, grow organically, sell to another mutual, or convert to a stock corporation.

Mutual banks that find organic growth difficult, or that have managers that tire of the business, need to find another mutual with an acquisitive appetite and ample capital, something rare in the mutual world. Mutual banks are restricted to merging only with other mutuals.

Another issue is mutual banks aren't allowed to raise outside capital. The capital they have to work with is the result of what they've started with originally, plus whatever retained earnings they've managed to accumulate.

MUTUAL CONVERSIONS

Over time, some mutuals desired to grow quicker than their deposit base allowed. The only way to do this was by converting from a mutual institution into a stock institution via an IPO. This was very popular in the 1980s and 1990s which was in some respects the golden era for mutual conversions (some like Peter Lynch of Fidelity fame made fortunes in this space). However, the IPO isn't a typical IPO (in fact, it's referred to as a "mutual conversion").

A mutual bank has no stock and is owned by its depositor members. When management decides to conduct an IPO they give preference rights on buying the new public shares to depositors first. There are no existing shareholders selling out and no dilution. Depositors who become shareholders are effectively getting "free" money in the IPO process.

The easiest way to understand a mutual conversion is by way of analogy. Imagine there are three friends who start a lawn mowing business during the summer (hopefully these are school-age kids, but we won't judge). They all own an equal share of the business which starts with a mower and just enough money for some gas. The three friends mow lawns all summer without distributing earnings so their mowing kitty grows and grows.

At the end of the summer the friends speak to a financial advisor they met at the local burger joint. In the meeting they decide they have been so successful that they'd like to convert their simple business arrangement to an ownership structure complete with shares.

Before the conversion to an ownership structure the mowing friends had $9,000 in cash earned from a summer's worth of hard work. As part of the conversion the friends decide that each of them needs to buy in with $3,000 to maintain their current stake. Each of them scrounges for the cash and contributes it to the new entity. Each friend now owns 1/3 of a company with $18,000 in equity, plus the mower and some gas for good measure.

This is a very rough analogy to a mutual conversion as the original depositors in a mutual -the ones who helped get the institution up and running - are usually long gone by the time of its IPO. As opposed to the example of the mowing group, it's depositor's capital, not sweat equity, that allowed the business to grow. But, the analogy is somewhat apt.

Investors coming in at the time of (or soon after) the IPO benefit because many of these mutuals convert at amounts as low as 60% or 70% of book value. This is due to the mechanics of the IPO structure whereby capital is contributed to an already capitalized institution. It's like buying a business and arriving to find a drawer full of cash someone had forgotten about. The "windfall" can be used to further grow the business or to simply put in your pocket (note that there are restrictions – see below - on timing and amounts of cash that can be taken out of a mutual following its IPO).

In the 1980s and 1990s – and even still today - investors would attempt to open deposit accounts in order to gain a toehold for the IPO. Many of these IPOs would shoot up 20-30% or more in the first few days of trading rewarding short term depositors (and any other lucky participants) with the capital to take advantage.

Unfortunately, the golden age of mutual conversions has effectively passed. The "easy" money has been made. There are still a few hundred mutual banks left in the U.S., but most are tiny and obscure, not ripe fruit hanging low on the branch just waiting to be picked. A few mutuals do convert each year, and the mechanics of the conversions haven't changed, but few of these IPOs have the same first day pop that they did in years past.

Mutual conversions are the net-nets of the banking world. A net-net is a stock with a market cap that's less than the value of the company's current assets (giving no effect to non-current assets like real estate, factory equipment and so forth) minus all liabilities. A net-net is a company trading for less than their expected liquidation value. In essence the market has decreed that a company like this is better off dead than alive.

A bank that has converted from being a mutual institution to a publicly traded stock institution is similar in many ways to a net-net. Often, the bank will start its trading life for significantly less than book value (much of it made up of cash and equivalents). This is a presumably low value for an institution which could, at least theoretically, close its doors and distribute much more than was paid for its shares.

A criticism about many mutual bank conversions is that the banks are small and typically unprofitable. Out of the 539 mutual banks in the U.S. at the end of 2015, the average quarterly net income was $607,000 (yes, $607 *thousand*, not million) with an average asset size of $814m. The majority of these mutuals are on the East Coast, with Massachusetts leading the pack at 99. More than half of these banks are located in Massachusetts, Ohio, Pennsylvania, New York, New Jersey, and Illinois.

Our humble opinion, which readers may choose to ignore, is that given the current state of play in the mutual arena investors who are interested in mutual conversions are better served by looking at them post-conversion rather than attempting to open deposit accounts and pray for an IPO.

An odd quirk of mutual conversions involves the restrictions on what corporate actions the newly converted entities are permitted to take. For example, converted mutual banks are not allowed to pay dividends, buyback shares or merge with other institutions outside of guidelines set by regulators. A converted institution can begin to buyback stock or pay dividends on the first anniversary of their conversion. On the third anniversary they are allowed to sell or merge the bank.

Some of the best investments in conversions are at former mutual banks with aging executives. The executives see an IPO as their exit strategy and a way to cash out and fund their retirement.

Mutual Holding Companies

Mutual banks might be confusing, but mutual holding companies (MHCs) are a whole different ball of enchiladas. An MHC is a combination of a mutual bank and a public bank holding company and is sometimes considered a partially converted mutual. So what is this strange beast known as an MHC?

An MHC is unleashed on the world when the management at a mutual bank decides they would like some public market exposure, but don't want to fully convert. What results is a mix of a public entity and a mutual.

The mutual bank creates an MHC that in turn owns the mutual bank. Another holding company is created which issues shares to the public, but not all of its shares. The public holding company owns a portion of the MHC and the MHC in turn owns the bank.

The MHC structure can be difficult to understand, but it also masks for investors the potential for hidden value. If an MHC wishes to fully convert they need to IPO the non-public portion of their holding company and fully convert the underlying bank into a stock owned bank. This is known as a "second step conversion". The mechanics of the conversion are the same as a mutual bank conversion. Depositors are given the opportunity to buy shares in the bank.

The wrinkle is that with an MHC there are public shareholders too. Public shareholders are issued new shares on pro rata basis designed to preserve their ownership interest. When an MHC conducts a second step conversion the capital from the IPO is injected into the entity.

Shareholders benefit from this arrangement as they own the same proportion of a bank with more equity post-transaction. Like straightforward mutual conversions, shareholders in an MHC can find themselves owners of a bank that is better capitalized at a lower valuation - something the market is supposed to price out. Investors who are able to navigate the complexities of the MHC structure can take advantage of second step conversions before the market even realizes what has happened.

TRADED BANKS WITHOUT HOLDING COMPANIES

There are over 1,200 publicly traded banks in the U.S., the vast majority of which are subsidiaries of bank holding companies (which, in most cases, is the public entity as opposed to the subsidiary bank). As discussed earlier, there are many advantages for a bank to utilize a bank holding company structure. Yet, even with these advantages there are a few hundred banks that trade on the open market without a parent holding company at all. The advantages to a bank not utilizing a bank holding company are simplicity and reduced costs, both of which in this context only make sense for very small institutions.

A bank holding company incurs additional regulation at the Federal level regardless of how simple the holding company is. The holding company also has its own corporate housekeeping requirements such as separate board meetings, accounting and bookkeeping. These might seem like minor expenses, but they add up and can be time consuming. For small banks where senior management is heavily involved in the day to day operations of the business, any hour not spent originating new loans is money lost. In addition, many of these small banks have by definition small asset bases and just can't afford the additional costs associated with a holding company.

There are also disadvantages for a bank that doesn't have a parent holding company. The first is that banks are subject to a more stringent level of regulation compared to bank holding companies. For example, banks require regulatory approval before paying dividends and buying back shares. This is because bank regulators are focused on the safety and soundness of a bank from the standpoint of depositors and not with a view to stockholders. A bank that is engaged in activities that could reduce capital is viewed as potentially imperiling the safety and soundness of the bank.

Investors should be aware of the advantages and disadvantages of banks that trade publicly without holding companies. A bank without a holding company is less flexible in what they can do in the marketplace, but they also have a lower cost burden associated with being public. So there are competing interests to consider and analyze.

S-Corporation Banks

The most familiar corporate structure in the United States is the C-Corporation (known, per the applicable provisions of the tax code, as a "C-Corp"). A C-Corp is an entity that is owned by shareholders, but is by law separate and distinct from them. A C-Corp pays its own taxes and its shareholders only pay taxes on dividends received from the company.

There is another lesser known corporate structure that offers some of the same legal protections to shareholders as a C-Corp - mainly limited liability - with a much more efficient tax structure. But, the tax efficiency of the S-Corporation (known, per the applicable provisions of the tax code, as a "S-Corp") structure doesn't come without some strings attached. The easiest way to think of an S-Corp is as a simplified C-Corp.

Like a C-Corp, an S-Corp is a separate legal entity, but it's a pass-through vehicle. This means that all profits and tax liability "pass through" to shareholders and there is no entity (corporate) level tax. Shareholders receive a Schedule K-1 from the company and report their proportionate share of income and deductions on their personal tax returns. Since income is only taxed once at the individual shareholder level (and not twice as with C-Corps), depending on personal tax rates the S-Corp tax burden can be significantly lower than that of a C-Corp.

There are two primary issues with S-Corp institutions. The first is that shareholders are liable for their share of taxes even if the company doesn't distribute any income. For example, imagine an S-Corp bank shareholder with a 25% ownership interest in a bank that earned $100 for the year. The shareholder would be required to report $25 in income on their personal taxes. If the S-Corp bank didn't distribute any of the $100 in income to shareholders, the shareholder would need to come up with the necessary tax payments out of their own savings or income.

The second and much larger issue for an S-Corp is the legal restrictions on how many shareholders the company can have. An S-Corp is limited to no more than 100 shareholders and, in addition, each shareholder needs to be a U.S. citizen or resident and a natural person (i.e. real live, breathing people as opposed to entities). The shareholder restrictions mean that not only can't funds own S-Corp banks, but other banks can't buy a piece of an S-Corp bank either.

The shareholder restrictions, as well as the potential tax headaches, have kept the pool of S-Corp banks small. It's not easy for investors to buy shares in an S-Corp bank as they are in essence buying a piece of a private company.

Unless an investor is looking to buy a private bank it's unlikely they'd ever even encounter an S-Corp bank. That is, until a very strange corporate transaction occurred in 2015.

North State Bancorp was a publicly traded North Carolina bank holding company. The bank had some credit issues during and after the financial crisis, but recovered and was experiencing growth. During that time, shares traded significantly below book value, but quickly appreciated.

In 2015, management issued a press release stating that they intended to convert the bank holding company from a C-Corp to an S-Corp. Their stated reason for doing this conversion was that the reduced tax burden of an S-Corp would enable them to pay out more of their income in the form of dividends.

To complete the transaction the company cashed out small shareholders (to get under the head count restrictions) and issued a series of preferred stock to finance the deal. Bank management also went to great lengths to screen investors who wished to continue owning their shares due to concerns about compliance with the law.

It's unknown whether the North State Bancorp transition from a public C-Corp to an S-Corp is the start of a trend for small banks or whether it was a one-off situation. Regardless, investors should be aware that the S-Corp structure exists and that some banks utilize it. This is an important distinction to make when comparing the tax burden between potential bank investments.

SUMMARY

One doesn't need to be an expert in banking structures to invest in banks. The most common structure in the industry is that of a bank holding company with a bank subsidiary. However, for every rule there are exceptions, and in this chapter we tried to cover the most common structural exceptions. Not only are these structures worth knowing for the sake of understanding, but often potential investment opportunities present themselves shrouded in a strange structure because other investors don't have the time or inclination to understand.

Now that we've covered the basics of banks at a high level it's time to dive into the nitty gritty beginning with financial statements in the next chapter.

8 FINANCIAL STATEMENT WALK-THROUGH

There is an expression that says that one "can't see the forest for the trees," which means that one is so focused on the details of a problem or issue that they miss the big picture. The expression is certainly fitting for many bank analysts who get hung up on trying to figure out what the incremental margin improvement will be on postage and office supplies in the next quarter.

Successful bank investors certainly pay attention to the trees, but they don't forget to consider the forest as a whole. This chapter is our chance to stare at some trees, otherwise known as details, and see how they fit into the wider picture. It's time to dig into the nitty gritty of a bank's financial statements.

Think of the financial statements as the framework for building an investment decision. Without a solid foundation it doesn't matter if your house has beautiful wainscoting, the whole thing can fall apart. The financial statements help ascertain risk, understand operations and provide investors the information they need to decide whether they want to add a certain bank to their investment portfolio.

In the United States, companies that are required to file their financial statements with the SEC must do so in accordance with Generally Accepted Accounting Principles (GAAP). There are four financial statements, which consist of (1) the balance sheet, (2) the income statement, (3) the cash flow statement and (4) the statement of shareholders' equity. However, for purposes of the basics of bank investing, the primary financials are the balance sheet and income statement and those are the two we will discuss in this chapter.

BALANCE SHEET

Most businesses and investors tend to focus on profits and corresponding profitability as reported on a company's income statement. There's nothing inherently wrong with that, but in some circumstances it can be misleading. At the very least it may paint an inaccurate picture of the state of play with respect to a given company.

For banks, while a profit is certainly important (who doesn't want to make money?) it all begins and ends with the balance sheet. A bank's profits are derived from their balance sheet. A bank with a bad balance sheet will have poor results and won't be able to earn enough to survive and weather a financial crisis. Even if survival isn't at issue, a bad balance sheet will virtually ensure that a bank can't earn it's cost of capital.

Think of a bank as a machine, a continuous machine that takes in deposits, makes loans with those funds and receives interest and ultimately the return of principal on those loans. The balance sheet is a snapshot of this machine frozen in place. It reflects the bank's financial position as of a single point in time. The bank's other financial statements capture the flow of the machine over a given period, but the balance sheet is always as of a single point in time. This is important to remember, and this is why investors can never solely rely on a balance sheet alone for an investment decision.

Investors used to looking at financial statements for non-financial companies often come away with the impression that a bank's balance sheet is confusing at best, and misleading at worst. Remember the discussion earlier on the view of banks' balance sheets as "black boxes".

But there's nothing to be scared of. We'll first look at the general structure of a bank's balance sheet and then dive into the details. As we move forward one thing to keep mind is that the balance sheet for a bank is "backwards" in the sense that most cash on hand (deposits) is a liability, while loans are an asset.

The general structure of a bank's balance sheet is as follows:

Assets	
	Cash
	Marketable Securities
	Loans
	Other assets such as branch buildings
	Other real estate owned (OREO)
Liabilities	
	Customer deposits
	Other funding sources
	• FHLB Advances
	• Debt
Equity Capital	
	Retained equity
	Preferred stock

A balance sheet must by definition balance, and a bank's balance sheet is no different. This means that the sum of the assets must equal the sum of the liabilities plus equity capital. It's two halves of the same coin in the sense that the liabilities and equity capital have been used or applied towards the purchase or acquisition of assets.

Let's tackle each item in the balance sheet one by one starting from the top.

Assets

CASH AND MARKETABLE SECURITIES

The easiest assets of a bank to understand are cash and marketable securities.

The bank pays interest on deposits monthly (or sometimes daily) and almost continuously receives principal and interest payments on their loans. If the institution is large enough they might be originating new loans nearly continuously as well as receiving loan payoffs at the same rate.

The cash for these transactions circulates through the bank's general account. A bank as an operating business needs to have readily accessible and liquid cash on hand to give to customers that withdraw money or for purposes of originating new loans, among many other things.

Banks generally have a target for the amount of cash they like to keep on hand. It's a moving, not absolute, target which can change depending on market and funding conditions. If a bank generated a balance sheet daily one would see this cash amount change from day to day, sometimes dramatically.

Banks certainly need cash to operate, but too much cash is inefficient, especially in today's low interest rate world. When rates are low cash generates little to no return outside of funding immediate operating activities.

A bank might need a sizable amount of cash occasionally, but not daily. So what do they do with that cash? They usually invest it in marketable securities which can range from ultra safe short term Treasury bonds to riskier longer dated mortgage-backed securities (MBS) and everything in between.

Rarely will a bank hold any meaningful amount of public equity securities. Until the early 20th Century it was very common for a bank to own an equity portfolio. Bankers would speculate in the market with their customer's deposits. Both the speculation and public equity positions caused significant issues when the market crashed in 1929. Bankers had gambled with their deposits and lost. When their customers came looking for their money there was none to be had.

Everyone probably remembers the scene from the movie *It's a Wonderful Life* where there was a run on the bank and not enough cash on hand. Because of this experience (the market crash, not *It's a Wonderful Life*) regulators predictably soured on banks owning public equities.

It's important to remember that while bank management is responsible for allocating capital they are not running a hedge fund inside a bank. If public equity securities show up on a bank's balance sheet in any meaningful amount it is something to pay particular attention to.

The majority of banks that investors will spend their time looking at will own a portfolio consisting of bonds.

Bonds are a natural fit for bankers since they are another form of what they're already doing, extending credit. A bond is an obligation in security form by a creditor to pay back a predetermined amount of principal plus interest over a fixed duration. The longer the duration of the bond, everything else being equal, the higher the interest rate. For example a bond maturing in one year might pay 1% per annum (in today's low interest rate environment), whereas a bond maturity in 10 years might pay 3% annually.

An average bank will have a mix of securities ranging from shorter term Treasury bonds to some longer dated MBS or even CDOs (collateralized debt obligations).

A general rule of thumb is the smaller the bank the more conservative they are with their securities portfolio (it's not always true, but that's why it's a rule of thumb and not a fact set in stone!). Small banks don't have the time or resources to analyze and evaluate a vast array of bonds in addition to their day to day business activities. In addition, smaller banks usually don't have all that much excess cash that needs to be put to work.

Although a paradox does exist. There is a relatively insignificant, but growing number of small banks that, especially in today's low interest rate environment, have trouble maintaining and growing their loan book. This contingent is extremely overcapitalized and invests most of their assets in fixed income securities which usually yield less than what they could receive from lending money.

LOANS

The largest item on the asset side of the ledger for a bank is (or should be – see above) loans receivable. These are loans made by the bank as a lender to customers who are borrowing various amounts at various durations. As noted above, a loan is an asset for a bank as opposed to a liability. By extending loans the bank expects a return on that money in the form of interest followed by the eventual repayment of principal. A more extensive discussion of loans and lending is found in the next chapter.

BANK BRANCHES

A traditional bank consists of one or more physical branch locations. Most of these are freestanding or located in a strip mall or sometimes even within a store, such as a Wal-Mart. In adapting to the internet age banks are closing branches at a record pace (in fact there are some banks without any physical locations at all), but that doesn't mean that their branches have no value. Bank branches can be sold for the building, the land or both, although it's often difficult to repurpose a bank branch into another type of business. Freestanding branches are built with banking in mind, usually with a drive-thru and a custom designed building that screams "I was born to be a bank!"

Even if a bank's branch is unlikely to be repurposed it still holds value and earns a place on the balance sheet. Remember, a balance sheet is the raw material that allows a bank to generate earnings. Bank branches are part of that raw material.

OTHER REAL ESTATE OWNED

The last item to discuss on the asset side of the balance sheet is the real estate owned by the bank (other than bank branches and related properties) which is typically known as "Other Real Estate Owned" (or "OREO", yes, like the cookie). OREO is a classification for real estate that a bank has taken possession of through foreclosure. This is the actual dirt and related structures as opposed to the loan itself. When the economy is doing well a bank's OREO account will usually be minimal, but when the economy slows down OREO values can balloon. This can also occur in more narrow circumstances such as bad lending decisions or a sector downturn (like energy) which are separate from the economy as a whole.

The OREO account merits extra attention from an investor because it can be a source of major issues for a bank. Let's consider the following example. A bank makes a $80,000 loan to Bob Builder to purchase a house for $100,000. Bob has 20% equity in the house resulting in a 80% loan to value ratio (LTV) for the bank.

Bob makes payments consisting of interest and principal for a period of time and reduces the outstanding balance of the loan to $70,000 (from $80,000). Bob then hits a rough patch and can no longer keep his loan current so the bank initiates foreclosure proceedings and seizes the house. In theory, the bank now owns a $100,000 asset that can be resold to satisfy the $70,000 obligation from the Bob, as the borrower. In a perfect world that would be true, but we don't live in a perfect world where one can simply travel to a mysterious island that looks a heck of a lot like Hawaii and have your every fantasy come true.

A borrower doesn't typically default on a mortgage when the housing market is strong and home values are rising. Borrowers default when the economy is troubled and home values are falling. This means the house Bob Builder bought for $100,000 might only resell in a bad market for $80,000 or even less.

Once the bank has the mortgage loan on its books (i.e. it now owns it as OREO), they have all the obligations and responsibilities of home ownership. This includes everything from ensuring taxes are timely paid to keeping the property maintained. This means they need to hire someone to mow the lawn, clear snow and make repairs, in each case as necessary.

Most banks are not in the business of managing a real estate portfolio and usually they want to get out from under their OREO as quickly as possible. Anyone with real estate experience knows that time to sale and maximizing value are in most cases mutually exclusive. That is, if you want to sell a house quickly you need to lower the price drastically. If you want to maximize the price received on the property it will take a long time to sell (or longer anyway). Consider the example again, our bank with its $100,000 face value loan on a house that's now worth $80,000 might need a further discount to ensure a quick sale. Perhaps that means selling the house for $70,000 or even less, thus incurring a loss on the property.

While a bank could decide to hold out for a higher price, no banker wants to be a part-time landlord for a real estate portfolio. Waiting has to be balanced against the obligations and responsibilities of real estate ownership noted above, as well as the fact that any money tied up in real estate isn't generating a return (and given the almost certain bad environment likely never will). Even worse for the bank, the OREO account generates a negative return due to carrying costs of ownership. Banks have a very strong incentive to liquidate OREO as fast as possible, even if that means taking a loss on the sale.

OTHER ASSETS

A bank might have certain additional assets other than what's discussed here, such as mortgage serving rights or the cash surrender value of life insurance policies, but those tend to be less significant to the overall evaluation and are beyond the scope of what is discussed here.

Liabilities

A liability is something that is owed to someone else. Why would a company want to undertake the obligation to owe something to someone? Because they get to use that "something" to generate earnings.

Banks take in deposits from customers and then turn around and lend those funds out to borrowers. Customer deposits can be a huge source of strength for a bank. A bank that can successfully acquire cheap and "sticky" deposits (i.e. deposits from customers who expect little in interest that are unlikely to walk quickly out the door for a little extra interest) can gain an advantage over competitors. Banks without strong deposit networks struggle to fund their daily operations.

CUSTOMER DEPOSITS

Deposits can be broadly grouped into two categories: time deposits and demand deposits. Both of these will be covered in detail later in the book. But for now let's hit the high points regarding this unusual source of funding.

In a traditional business there are current liabilities and long-term liabilities. Current liabilities are liabilities due within the next year, while long-term liabilities are due more than a year in the future. Current liabilities usually consist of items such as short-term debt funding or accounts payable. Whereas, long-term liabilities are things such as bonds or loans with a maturity date after the one year mark and pension liabilities.

A bank doesn't segregate their liability accounting into short-term and long-term obligations. They are unable to since it isn't clear at a detailed enough level to segregate their liabilities in such a manner.

When a customer puts money on deposit at a bank they have to choose what type of account they would like. They can choose between different products, such as a checking account, a savings account, or a certificate of deposit. In any of these types of accounts the money is on deposit at the bank only so long as the customer desires.

Banks attempt to manage the duration of deposits through a variety of deposit products. A demand deposit is a deposit that can be redeemed by a customer at any time. Think of this as similar to a traditional current liability.

Time deposits are products which lock up a customer's funds for a specified amount of time. Often the maturities in these types of products are longer than a year. Banks attempt to lock up funds in CDs with stipulations on the product. A customer can cash out a CD earlier than the maturity date, but they end up paying an early redemption fee or being penalized to the tune of a few months worth of interest.

Think of a time deposit as similar to a non-current asset. In general, a bank's demand deposits are a cheaper source of funding compared to time deposits. When a bank can't attract sufficient deposits they are forced to rely on other funding sources.

OTHER FUNDING SOURCES

A bank without a strong deposit network that wants to support loan growth has to look at alternate funding sources. The most common source of non-deposit funding for a bank is via subordinated debt.

When a non-bank needs capital they generally take on debt in the form of a bank loan. But banks don't typically loan to other banks in order to support their lending. Banks take on debt by selling notes into the market or to private investors.

Bank notes are often simple securities. For example, they might carry a fixed maturity date with a coupon. The bank pays investors who purchase the notes the coupon through the date of maturity, at which time the bank repays the principal.

The last source of funding that is worth mentioning is the issuance of preferred stock. Preferred stock is a type of equity with preference rights over common equity.

Most banks issue preferred stock that is perpetual in nature. That is, there is no fixed maturity for the preferred stock. The stock is senior in liquidation preference to equity holders, and preferred holders usually receive a fixed dividend on their shares.

LIABILITY PECKING ORDER

When evaluating a bank's liability structure it's worth keeping in mind a simple liability pecking order:

Demand deposits → Time deposits → Subordinated Debt → Preferred Stock

EQUITY CAPITAL

A discussion of the balance sheet wouldn't be complete without a few words about the bank's equity capital.

Equity is the difference between a bank's assets and their liabilities. If a bank has $100 in assets and $30 in liabilities they have $70 in equity capital.

Bank investors tend to speak of equity as if it was a "thing". Equity isn't a specified set of earmarked assets sitting in the vault ready to be utilized, it's just the simple difference between assets and liabilities.

Regulatory capital requires a different analysis where regulators only count certain assets to be applied toward a capital position. This is discussed further in Chapter 12

INCOME STATEMENT

The income statement reflects a company's financial performance, such as its revenue, expenses and profitability (or lack thereof). While the balance sheet is a snapshot of a single point in time, the income statement measures financial performance over a certain period of time (such as a quarter or year).

A bank's income statement, in banking terms, is essentially a measure of the bank's ability to capture a spread by lending money at a higher rate than the sum of its cost of deposits/borrowing and operating costs.

The general structure of a bank's income statement is shown on the next page.

Interest income
Interest expense
Net interest income
Provision for loan losses
Noninterest income
Noninterest expense
Profit before income taxes
Income taxes
Net income

INTEREST INCOME

At its most basic level, a bank is in the business of taking in deposits and lending those funds out with the expectation and hope that agreed upon interest will be paid at the designated times and the money will be repaid at the designated maturity. If these amounts exceed expenses (i.e. capturing the spread, as described above) then the bank will make money.

When a borrower makes a payment on a loan the interest portion of the payment appears on the bank's income statement as interest income received. Interestingly, it's only the interest portion of the payment that is reported on the income sheet, not any principal repayment amounts. This is because the principal is a repayment of the bank's own money and is not income.

Imagine a situation where you lend a friend $20 if they

will give you $25 back in a month. Hey, the person is a friend, but you're a good capitalist and want to make some money too. A month later the unicorn friend (since they're the only friend in the history of the world who has ever repaid a small loan) gives you the agreed upon $25. $20 of the amount is your return of principal, while the additional $5 is interest income.

So in the balance sheet of your life, the $20 would be reflected on the balance sheet while the $5 would run through the income statement (and eventually affect the balance sheet as well).

INTEREST EXPENSE

In order to have money to lend out, banks need a source of funding. Of all the available options, customer deposits are the cheapest form of funding and has been discussed in detail earlier in the book. Bank customers are typically not a greedy group and with many types of bank products customers have come to expect little to no interest on the deposits they place at a bank. Especially in today's low interest rate world, depositors are receiving next to nothing on their deposited amounts.

If banks had their druthers (because everyone wants druthers), they would finance themselves completely via deposits, but that's not always possible. If a bank wants to grow their lending book beyond their ability to do so with their deposit base, they would need to raise funds by issuing debt or preferred stock or borrowing money from their Federal Home Loan Bank or elsewhere. Any interest paid on deposits or borrowings is classified as an interest expense.

NET INTEREST INCOME

THE BANK INVESTORS HANDBOOK

Net interest income is the difference between the amount of interest income the bank receives and the amount of interest expense the bank pays or incurs. Perhaps the most popular way of calculating this measure of profitability is by looking at a bank's net interest margin (NIM) which is the difference between the income earned on interest-earning assets (i.e. loans) and interest expense incurred on liabilities (i.e. deposits and borrowed funds) to carry those assets, expressed as a yield.

Banks are regularly compared to one another based on their NIM. All else being equal, the higher the NIM the better performing the bank. This is because the NIM is the best measure of the bank's largest operating endeavor, which is the ability to generate a return on their lending activities. Banks with a strong NIM are operating from a position of strength, they have more resources available to fund operations and are not as reliant on non-interest income to generate a profit.

PROVISION FOR LOAN LOSSES

The provision for loan losses is a contra account found on the balance sheet. That is, it's simply a reserve for expected or anticipated losses on outstanding loans. Periodically a bank will review their loan book and analyze whether they expect (based on certain criteria) to receive the contracted principal and interest on each loan. To the extent they determine a loss might be suffered, they are required to reserve funds to cover that loss. If and when losses are incurred the loan loss reserve account is reduced.

When the economy hits a rough patch and losses are anticipated, one will often see the allowance for loan losses increasing dramatically quarter over quarter. As losses are realized this amount is reduced. There is a timing disconnect between when the funds are reserved via the income statement and when they are actually applied at a later date. Often you'll see that there has been an excess of reserves put away and they are "released" when things improve.

When reserves are released they end up on the income statement increasing net income and, thus, distorting profitability. A well run bank will slightly over-reserve in good years as a protection against bad years. Poorly run banks will swing wildly between under-reserved (resulting in a scramble to cover bad loans) and then over-reserved (pushing them to release excess reserves). When a bank is in a cycle of under-reserving they are like a ticking time bomb. They might be able to weather minor crises, but a major one will ruin them.

An interesting side note is that when a bank releases excess reserves (and, thus, increases profitability) analysts and the media will loudly claim that the bank's numbers are skewed and "fake". However, one will never hear the opposite; that a bank's numbers are being too negatively hit by needing to add to reserves, even if later they're not needed.

This discussion wouldn't be complete without noting that regulations on reserves are poised to change. In the future, when implemented, banks will be required to determine if they expect a loan to suffer a loss at the time of origination and set aside reserves at that time.

If this seems like a paradox, it's because it is. If a bank expected a loan to suffer a loss they wouldn't originate it. At the time of origination no bank thinks a loan will go bad. But the regulators in their infinite wisdom feel that this change should protect against future banking crises.

Noninterest Income

A bank's non-interest income line item on the income statement encompasses any additional income the bank generates outside of interest from its lending activities (which also includes dividends received on its investment securities book). This could be anything from overdraft fees, fees for investment management services, mortgage servicing fees, credit card lending fees, and any gains (or losses) from sales of securities or other property. Any income received from other non-banking businesses owned by the holding company will be found here.

Since the Great Recession in 2008 banks have struggled with the low interest rate environment. Remember that the bulk of a typical bank's income comes from interest earned on loans. The lower interest rates are, the less they can charge for a loan. Some of this is balanced by a lower cost of funding, but it usually isn't enough.

In response to low rates many banks have attempted to increase their non-interest income. Some attempts have run afoul of banking regulators. For example, at one point certain banks decided to re-order customer transfers from the largest such amount to the smallest in an attempt to ensure those customers triggered an overdraft with related fees. Other banks have added monthly service fees to accounts if certain requirements aren't met, such as one direct deposit and three debit transactions per month. If there is a system that can be gamed there will be people gaming it, and non-interest income from fees is no different.

Non-Interest Expense

In a typical case, the majority of non-interest expenses

for a bank are their operating costs. Operating expenses are a large category. In theory, anything that's needed to operate the business can fall into this bucket. Operating expenses consist of anything and everything related to operating the business from employee salaries, rent, marketing and information technology costs on down to the purchase of branded pens, tiny calendars and toasters (banks know that the way to their customers' wallets is through a good piece of properly toasted toast).

The largest non-interest expense is typically employee salaries. The larger the bank, the more personnel required to run the operation. At a single branch bank employees might consist of a few tellers, a loan officer or two, and a small management team. At a larger bank the more specialized positions become with such areas as dedicated IT and regulatory/compliance departments. When a bank is looking to cut costs the lowest hanging fruit is employee compensation which is done through branch closures and direct layoffs.

Another considerable expense for banks is information technology. A bank no longer keeps its cash in the vault, it is now held on digital ledger books. Customers have come to expect online banking, remote check deposit and the ability to conduct all banking activity directly from their smartphone. These technology expectations and advances have real costs and the larger the bank the more complex and costly it is.

INCOME TAXES

In theory, a bank's taxes should be a straightforward calculation of their income before taxes multiplied by the appropriate tax rate. But like everything in banking, it's not quite that simple. A bank's tax rate is driven by a variety of factors, which includes the amount of previous tax losses the bank has carried forward and the composition of taxable income.

The amount of losses a bank can carry forward to offset future income (and, thus, income taxes) is a complicated subject. GAAP accounting often doesn't match up with accounting for income tax purposes. For example, a bank might be allowed from an income tax perspective to recognize excess depreciation that GAAP rules don't permit. There can also be simple timing differences between GAAP and tax accounting. In these situations a deferred tax asset (DTA) or deferred tax liability (DTL) might appear on a company's balance sheet.

If a bank had considerable losses previously it might be recognized as a DTA. The DTA is slowly used up as a bank returns to profitability where prior losses offset current income and taxable liability is reduced.

Likewise, in some situations a bank is able to postpone the payment of specific taxes well into the future which results in a DTL. Some banks are so masterful with the use of DTLs that they have created a situation where their DTL will never be paid. Some academics believe that when it appears a DTL will never be paid it should be considered as part of the company's equity. Bank regulators disagree with this approach and believe it is inappropriate for a bank.

A note of caution for investors when including a DTL as equity. Remember that the current state of affairs might not continue on forever. It's possible that the DTL will eventually come due and the value of what you thought you owned will be reduced.

NET INCOME

A bank's net profit or net income is what's left over after subtracting all expenses and taxes from their net interest income and non-interest income. It is vital for a bank to become and remain profitable in order to stay in business for more than a few years. The level of profitability is the ultimate touchstone for how effective a bank's operations are and is a measure of its success.

The net income a bank earns in one year becomes excess cash and additional capital for the next year. This can be seen via an increase in shareholders' equity (due to an increase in retained earnings). This extra capital can be used to make more loans and support a larger organization. For a variety of reasons some banks have difficulty in growing their loan book, but if they are profitable they can at the very least buy growth through the acquisition of another bank.

This concludes our walk through of a bank's primary financial statements. The next few chapters will examine certain portions of a bank's financial statements in greater depth.

9 LENDING

A bank with a small loan book and a pile of cash and securities isn't much of a bank. They're really more of a bond fund in bank's clothing. Remember that at the most basic level banks are in the business of taking in deposits and making loans with those funds.

All banks make loans; the question is what are the terms and types of loans. A loan is documented as a contract between the bank, as lender, and a person or entity, as borrower. It provides that the bank will lend a certain amount of money to the borrower and that the borrower will repay those funds with interest at a certain time or times.

The bank will typically have certain agreed upon provisions in the agreement to protect it in case the borrower fails to make interest payments or repay the principal. This could be anything from foreclosing on collateral (if it's what's known as a "secured loan") or suing the borrower in court.

Many think of bank lending through the lens of *It's a Wonderful Life*. This is a world where getting a bank loan is like a visit to see George Bailey at the Bailey Building & Loan. The potential borrower visits the local bank and meets with a banker, who is a person they've known for years, and pleads their case as to why they are worthy to receive a loan. The banker then makes this loan, or doesn't, primarily on the basis of the character of the person.

Many of us retain this stereotype, but it doesn't resemble modern banking. Banks engage in a variety of different types of lending from residential lending to consumer lending to commercial lending.

Lending by Type (2017 Q2)	
1-4 Family residential	20%
1-4 family construction	1%
Other construction	4%
Agricultural Production	1%
Farmland	2%
Commercial & Industrial	18%
Credit Cards	7%
Auto Lending	5%

The most basic issues regarding bank lending are how does a bank do it, and what are the important aspects of the process. The actual process is quite interesting.

TYPES OF LENDING

Bank lending is most often equated with residential lending. For many banks residential lending is a very significant and important component of bank lending, but it's not the only one. There are a number of different types of lending a bank might engage in. These include residential loans, commercial property loans, inventory loans, mezzanine financing, bridge loans, different forms of asset securitization, and on and on.

It would be impossible to cover every type of loan, especially some of the more esoteric specialty loans. Instead we'll talk about the most common loans and how to view them within the context of a bank's portfolio.

Before discussing how to evaluate a bank's loan portfolio, let's quickly review the various categories of lending a bank might engage in.

RESIDENTIAL LOANS

This is the most common type of bank lending. When a bank makes a loan to a borrower for purposes of purchasing a home (typically a primary residence) that is what is known as a residential loan.

In a traditional residential home purchase a person will directly or indirectly approach a bank and ask them if they are willing to make them a loan in order to purchase a property. The bank investigates the property and has it appraised. Then, they research the potential borrower, their sources and amount of income, how much they intend to borrow and their past borrowing history. If all of these items are satisfactory to the bank they will commit to make the loan which is typically secured by the property to be purchased. The borrower enters into a contract (a mortgage) with the bank promising to pay the full amount of the loan back with interest over a set duration.

The most common type of residential loan in the U.S. is the 30-year mortgage. With a 30-year mortgage the principal and interest are amortized over the duration of the loan with a fixed monthly payment. In the early years of the loan the homeowner's payment consists primarily of interest rather than principal. As the borrower pays down the loan over time this mix of principal and interest shifts to more of a reduction of principal than payment of interest.

There is no regulation that requires that mortgages must be 30 years in length, but this is the cultural standard in the U.S. In other countries, like Japan, longer mortgages such as those lasting 100 years are common and become essentially generational family obligations rather than individual obligations. The second most popular duration of mortgage in the U.S. is the 15-year mortgage, although it's possible to obtain a mortgage with virtually any duration so long as a bank is willing to come to terms with the borrower. As an example, one of your authors had a 20-year mortgage that was re-financed into a 12-year mortgage.

Less common is variable rate lending on primary residences, as well as balloon loans. A balloon loan is one where the payments are set low for a specified period of time with the entire loan principal amount coming due at a later date. For example, a borrower might obtain a $100,000 balloon loan with monthly payments of $250 per month for five years. Five years into the loan the entire principal would be due at once.

CONSUMER CREDIT LOANS

This is one of the most straightforward, but also riskiest, types of lending a bank can engage in. Consumer credit is made up of anything from credit card lending to direct unsecured loans of the type that are often used for the purpose of purchasing goods or services.

Consumer credit typically isn't secured (that is, there is no collateral) and is usually quickly discharged in a bankruptcy proceeding. Before the Great Financial Crisis it wasn't uncommon for a bank to send what looked like a check in the mail for a few thousand dollars. A consumer who wanted to use this money could sign the check and cash it. By doing so they were initiating a consumer loan with the bank, usually at a usurious interest rate. Banks were practically mailing money to people with the hope that a few would sign and pay a little bit of interest – enough interest to offset the inevitable defaults.

The primary reason a bank engages in consumer lending is that the interest rates are much higher than those of other types of loans. For example, the average credit card rate is over 15% but can reach well over 20% in some situations where a borrower has bad credit. The general approach with this type of lending is that the high interest rates will compensate the bank for the eventual (and expected) defaults from certain borrowers.

The general back of the napkin math works like this. A bank extends $100,000 in consumer credit loans at 18% interest. They expect 8% of those loans to default and be written off each year. They will earn approximately $16,560 in interest (18% x $100k minus the written off loans). Reduce this $16,560 in interest by $8,000 (the written off loans) and you have a portfolio that generated around an 8.6% return. Not too shabby.

Auto/Vehicle Lending

This is when a bank extends a loan to a borrower so they can purchase a vehicle. Typically, the loan will be secured by the purchased vehicle. Rates vary on these loans, but are usually a few points above the then-current prime rate.

Business/Commercial Loans (Including Real Estate)

A bank loan to a business or commercial entity is typically classified as a business or commercial loan. This type of lending can take many forms since each situation is different. A business might take out a loan to purchase inventory, for working capital, to fund a facilities expansion or for a variety of other reasons. A loan to a business for purposes of purchasing real estate (anything from an apartment building to a warehouse to an office tower) is called a commercial real estate loan.

Business/commercial loans usually carry higher interest rates than residential loans and often don't have a standard amortization schedule. For example, in the case of a commercial real estate loan, rather than amortize over say a 30 year period via principal and interest payments, a business might pay interest only with a balloon payment for the entire principal due at the end of the term. This is one of the reasons why banks can sometimes get in trouble with commercial real estate.

Construction Loans

This is when a bank extends a loan to a borrower that is usually secured by dirt (i.e. a piece of land without a structure on it). The size of the loan is sufficient to fund construction of a future building on the site, but at the time of the loan all that exists is land and hopes and dreams.

Construction loans are among the riskiest types of loans. This is because there is no physical property to be secured against, and in the case of a commercial property there might not be cash flow to support payments until the facility is complete and in use. This could take years.

OTHER TYPES

Other than the types of loans we've briefly discussed above, there are little niches of lending that various banks engage in. If there is a potential borrower who needs money, then usually there will be a bank willing to craft a loan to serve that need. Since this book is not called The Exhaustive Encyclopedia of Lending (although that's a good name for a book) we're going to cut our discussion short with a few thoughts on other types of loans.

For most banks, lending outside of the categories we've described is ancillary and makes up a small portion of their loan portfolio. In a few unusual cases there are banks that not only engage in, but specialize in, niche lending. This could be agricultural lending in California or Illinois to construction lending in Texas to "faith based" lending (loans to religious organizations) in the Southeast and everything in between.

If a bank makes a few small "other" loans it's not something worth spending a lot of time investigating. However, if a bank makes a specialty of niche lending an investor needs to spend time understanding how that niche lending works and any special risks associated with it. Usually this can be accomplished with some internet surfing, but if Ma Google fails a quick call to the bank is the best path to understanding their specific business.

LOAN UNDERWRITING

For those of a certain age, you may recall the 1976 Schoolhouse Rock segment, "I'm Just a Bill". Set against a groovy tune, kids (and adults who watch cartoons) learned the steps a bill must go through in order to become a law. Like a bill, loan origination is the beginning of the journey for a loan to be made.

Once a bank makes the decision to lend to a borrower they are effectively 'stuck' with that loan until one of three things occurs: either they sell it, it's paid off, or it defaults. Because of this, a bank needs to spend a lot of time and effort upfront to ensure that they are loaning money to what they believe is a good credit without many risks.

Historically, banks were in the business of asset-based lending. This means that banks would focus on the assets, or collateral, backing a loan. For example, if a loan was to be used for purposes of purchasing a residential property, the bank wanted a borrower to pay 20% of the purchase price in order to ensure some "skin in the game". The bank would then order an appraisal and satisfy itself that the value of the property exceeded their 80% stake in the purchase price. Thus, in a foreclosure situation the bank could seize the property and sell it for around the appraised value without suffering a loss.

The focus of the bank's analysis was on the hard asset value and not the income necessary to support the interest payments and, ultimately, the repayment of principal. From a value investor's perspective this is akin to focusing on the balance sheet rather than the income statement.

There are various issues with asset-based lending that are problematic. One problem is that collateral doesn't always have a fixed value. When a borrower begins to have trouble paying their loan it often coincides with a downturn in the economy or specific industry which results in a drop in related asset values.

In the Great Recession, for example, banks discovered that the appraised value of the residential properties they lent against had been propped up by a housing bubble and were simply unrealizable in any kind of normal market.

The same situation exists for business lending. A company's inventory or receivables aren't worth much if there is no demand for the inventory or if the receivables are also from troubled companies.

Another issue with asset-based loans is the time and resources that need to be dedicated to both policing collateral and seizing it if the need arises. If a loan is secured by widgets located in warehouses in 10 states, it's difficult if not impossible for the bank to periodically view the collateral and ensure that it's still sufficiently valuable. Likewise, what if a bank needs to foreclose on a loan to a steel company secured by acres of steel rolls? The costs involved in securing it, moving it and storing it are astronomical and, frankly, prohibitive and outside the scope of what most bank's are able to do.

As a result of these factors, among others, banks began to focus on cash flow and the ability to pay interest and principal in addition to, and perhaps more important than, asset values when lending. The value of collateral isn't as important if a borrower has the wherewithal to continue to make payments even when times are tough. Better to protect against default than worry about recovery values, if you will.

Credit card companies, for example, have always understood that it's the ability to make payments that matters, not any assets that back a loan (in fact, the vast majority of credit cards are unsecured). Inertia is a strong force and it creates an interesting dynamic for borrowers. A borrower is inclined to continue to make payments on their debt even if the assets that support it are worth less than the outstanding balance (or the loan isn't secured at all).

Commercial loan underwriting takes a somewhat different approach than residential loan underwriting. Some of this is due to the fact that the loans are generally quite a bit larger, but there's a different dynamic as well. When a bank contemplates a commercial loan the lending officer (also, called an "underwriter" in commercial terms) reviews financial statements from the company and analyzes the business's ability to make payments on the loan in different economic environments. This is referred to as "stress testing" the loan.

In addition, a commercial underwriter might hold extended discussions with management regarding the outlook for their business. The whole point is for the bank to be comfortable that the business is able to satisfy current interest payments and the ultimate repayment of principal. That's no different from a residential loan in a sense, but the focus of the analysis is on different things.

THE IMPORTANCE OF THE LENDING MIX

Ultimately, a bank's lending mix in terms of size, yield and industry will determine its profitability and related risk profile. Lending is a balancing act between loans that are potentially riskier, but yield more, versus loans that are perceived or deemed to be safer, but yield less. A bank also needs to balance the size of loans and borrower mix. A bank that goes "all-in" on riskier loans in an effort to increase their portfolio yield and interest income needs to either have a high loss reserve or a bankruptcy attorney on speed-dial.

An example of a riskier strategy was construction and development loans (C&D loans) leading up to the financial crisis. A C&D loan is a loan made to a real estate developer for purposes of buying and developing a piece of property, such as a new office building. These are typically short-term, high yielding loans. The risk is that the development never comes to fruition or once developed doesn't generate the expected earnings.

Recalling the discussion above, a commercial loan will usually depend to some extent on the success of the business. When the financial crisis came many developers not only couldn't make interest payment, but couldn't repay the principal when the loan came due. Adding insult to injury, the collateral (again, noting the discussion on asset-based loans above) wasn't of sufficient value and couldn't be sold at the time, at least not at any kind of acceptable price.

Getting the optimal loan mix correct is a high-wire act without a net. Bank officers are really loan portfolio managers. Savvy managers look at their portfolio on a blended basis and try to manage performance and risk. A portfolio that's too safe won't produce enough income, while a risky portfolio is, well, risky. The tricky aspect of managing a loan book is that a bad mix of loans might be anything from a concentration in large, risky C&D loans to lower yielding, long-dated residential loans.

The problem is there are a lot of potentially bad lending mixes. So instead, let's focus on what an ideal lending mix might look like. Note that this isn't *the* ideal lending mix, but simply *an* ideal lending mix.

In a perfect world a bank would want to have a large portion of their loan portfolio in commercial/business loans, which offer a number of advantages to a bank. They are larger in size, usually of short maturity and they carry a higher yield. Additionally, banks usually require business customers to keep a certain amount of cash in their deposit account at the bank to be held against the loan. In essence, the bank is requiring the business to put up a cash reserve against their own loan which is then re-lent back to themselves.

It's not only the nature of the loan that makes business lending profitable, it's also the relationship. For most, obtaining a loan in order to purchase a residential property is an infrequent occurrence. Maybe it happens a few times in one's life. The residential lending process is, thus, impersonal. Borrowers tend to shop around for their loan and simply go with whoever is the cheapest. Therefore, from the bank's perspective residential lending is a commodity business.

Business lending is different, it's relationship based on both sides. A business owner is most definitely looking for a good rate, but they also need good service. From the bank's standpoint, as opposed to residential lending, each situation is more unique and not fungible. As a result, a bank needs to be in frequent communication with a business to assess its credit quality on an ongoing basis.

The relationship with a company can lead to other business being done between the two parties. Perhaps there are more loans in the future. Perhaps a company can take advantage of a bank's asset management services or trust services if they have them. Maybe there's insurance needs. The point being that a good relationship can result in benefits to both the bank, in the form of additional business, and the borrower, in the form of a trusted service partner.

As the relationship grows, a bank's lending officer gets to know their business customers and can make judgments based on character and past history. Business lending officers are similar to stockbrokers in the sense that their clients often consider themselves as doing business with them and not the company they work for. It isn't unusual for a business lending officer to leave one bank for another and take the majority of their clients with them to the new bank. This happens because these business customers don't want to spend the time and energy developing a new relationship when the capital they need to run their company is at stake.

Most banks profess to have an interest in business lending, but run into problems if they don't have pre-existing relationships or the ability to hire suitable business lending officers. It's very difficult to create business lending relationships from scratch. What tends to happen in those situations is a bank will end up attracting clients from the wrong side of the tracks. These are businesses that either couldn't obtain credit at other banks or that are very price sensitive and willing to shop for rates (without caring much for the relationship aspect of things). Neither of these are desirable types of clients.

Some banks specialize in just business lending and, surprisingly to no one, they're called business banks. A business bank usually gets its start when business leaders from a community come together and form a bank to serve their needs. The bank has a pre-existing set of clients and these business leaders refer other businesses in their network. A business bank started by community business leaders is pre-seeded with the types of relationships it needs to grow and be successful.

ADDITIONAL DISCUSSION OF SPECIFIC RISKS IN LENDING

We've discussed many of the risks inherent in lending earlier in the book. However, we thought that a few additional points should be made or, in certain cases, emphasized.

The larger the loan, the more potential risk it carries. A pitfall to business lending is that when a loan starts to go bad it can sour very quickly. It's like that old saw about first going bankrupt slowly, then all at once. This is problematic because business loans tend to be larger than other types of loans. A single business loan might be the same size as as 10-20 residential loans at a small bank or thousands or even tens of thousands of residential loans at a regional or larger bank.

Banks need to be patient and work with the business borrower if they run into issues. Outside of a few rare cases the business borrower can only repay the loan if they are an operating entity since few business loans are made on an asset-based basis.

Another type of risk a bank incurs when lending money is interest rate risk. Interest rates are rarely static, they move up and down over time and all the time. Most bank lending is at a fixed rate meaning that the bank is locking in their rate of return over a specified period of time.

In a period of increasing rates long duration loans guarantee a bank sub-par returns. This is because as time passes the return from new money lent is higher than old money lent. In a rising rate environment banks attempt to delay lending as long as possible and keep their money in cash or short-term securities. When banks do lend they lend for shorter periods. It's unusual to find a bank making and holding a lot of 30 year loans in an increasing rate environment.

When rates are declining banks attempt to lend as much money as possible for as long as possible with the hope they can snag a few borrowers for the long term at lucrative yields. A problem for banks is that their borrowers aren't stupid and when rates fall they rush to refinance. It doesn't help that some banks position their entire business model on refinancing, advertise heavily and promote a race to the bottom with low rate lending.

There are many different strategies to mitigate interest rate risk, almost as many strategies as there are banks. Every banker will tell you that they have rates under control and know where they're going, but it's simply not true. But it is true that some have a good sense about rates. One banker told one of your authors (paraphrasing): "Everyone has been wrong on rates for the past 10 years, and everyone knows where they're headed now. They don't, and they never will. We take advantage of what we see today."

UNDERSTANDING A BANK'S LOAN BOOK

Even though there are thousands of banks in the US most banks have similar loan portfolio mixes, similar back office operations and, to some extent, are just variations of each other.

Banks tend to be similar in their lending practices in that they're either heavy residential lenders, business lenders, or well rounded regional or super regional lenders. Of course, there's the occasional niche lender as well. Investors, the media and anyone who talks about banking like to highlight the niche lenders because they're interesting.

There is nothing interesting about a small residential thrift bank that does the exact same thing that 2,000 other banks do. But for investors these patterns are useful. There are patterns to lending that make analyzing a bank's loan book easier.

The first place to look when analyzing a bank's loans is

the overall portfolio composition. What are the types of loans that a bank specializes in? Are they primarily a residential lender or an auto lender? The type of lending a bank engages in will determine the types of risks a bank is exposed to.

Strong arguments can be made as to whether it's better for a bank to be focused on doing one thing well, or being a well-rounded institution that does multiple things well enough. The argument for doing one thing well is that the bank will know their market better than most and can take advantage of opportunity in that specific segment. The argument for a well rounded bank is that different types of lending act as a diversifier and can help reduce risk, while at the same time enabling the bank to earn a slightly higher return.

Each situation is different. What matters is how the bank is executing within the model they've chosen. If a bank is a dedicated business lender, well are they a good business lender?

After examining the composition of a bank's portfolio an investor should look at the duration of the portfolio. A bank's portfolio maturity can be found in their Call Report, or through an online data provider such as CompleteBankData.com.

The following table shows a loan portfolio's maturity and repricing for State Bank and Trust Company of Greenwood, MS:

	2017 Q2	As % of Total
Maturity		
Three months or less	100,810	11.71%
Over three months through twelve months	70,587	8.20%
Over one year through three years	143,518	16.68%
Over three years through five years	197,168	22.91%
Over five years through fifteen years	152,324	17.70%
Over fifteen years	0	0.00%
Repricing		
Three months or less	12,116	1.41%
Over three months through twelve months	17,261	2.01%
Over one year through three years	36,830	4.28%
Over three years through five years	75,964	8.83%
Over five years through fifteen years	46,423	5.39%
Over fifteen years	475	0.06%
Loans and leases, gross	**860,521**	

As an investor you want to invest in banks that are positioned correctly for whatever the current rate environment is. No one knows the future, but a bank needs to pass the sniff test. If interest rates are at historic lows it doesn't make sense for a bank to be making mostly 30 year loans. A bank doing that wouldn't pass the sniff test. Correct positioning, or at least positioning similar to the rest of the market is an indication that bank management has a heartbeat and is vaguely aware of the market.

The next thing an investor wants to check is the quality of the bank's loans. We'll cover this in Chapters 9 and 14.

Beyond examining basic composition and maturity it's also important to view a bank's loan portfolio within the context of the rest of the business. A loan portfolio viewed in isolation could appear to be safe, but within the context of the entire bank very risky.

An example of this might be a bank making 30 year loans and financing it with hot money deposits. As discussed earlier, these are often CDs that pay higher coupons and where the depositors have no loyalty to the institution.

The last thing to consider is how the bank is financing their loan portfolio. Is it through low cost deposits, or is it through debt?

If a bank is financed with high cost deposits and debt it makes no sense for them to make barely profitable residential loans. The safest and lowest yielding loans should be made with low cost deposits, whereas potentially higher returning loans might justify the use of debt.

SUMMARY

There are a lot of moving pieces to a bank's loan portfolio, and this chapter just barely touches on the high points. But one thing to keep in mind is you don't need to be an expert in local real estate and know the address of every property a bank has lent against to make a judgment as to the quality of their lending.

The types of loans, the duration of those loans, the lending mix, as well as the historical performance, tell a story about a bank's management and the quality of their lending.

10 DEPOSITS

What makes a bank a bank? Is it their lending? No, that isn't what makes a bank a bank. There are numerous non-bank entities that engage in lending activities. It's the bank's deposits that set them apart from other financial institutions.

Bank deposits are in a sense a sacred trust. Customers give their money to a bank with the expectation that they will receive at least what they gave the bank back, if not slightly more (via interest payments). Customers aren't making an investment when they place their money in a deposit account. They view a bank as a place to safely keep their money until it's needed later.

The problem for customers is that while they don't view a bank deposit as an investment that's what it actually is. Money deposited at a bank is used by the bank to fund loans and purchase investment securities. There's a dramatic difference in expectations. Customers view deposits as a place to safely store their money and perhaps get a small bit of interest payments, whereas bankers view deposits as a funding source, the fuel for their lending engine.

One doesn't need to travel that far back in history to find examples where this expectation disconnect was laid bare. Where in times of economic crisis depositors suddenly woke up and realized that the bank that was holding their money wasn't a safe place to park cash after all as it was gambling with customer deposits.

It's when this realization happens that customers en masse flood the bank in an attempt to withdraw their funds on deposit at the same time. This is the oft feared "run on the bank." The problem for a bank is that they only have a tiny fraction of their customers deposits on hand. The rest of the deposits are in longer term investments, loans and investment securities. Once depositors withdraw the cash on hand, a bank finds themselves in a liquidity crisis without funds to operate.

One of your authors (Nate) remembers being a kid and opening his first bank account with his parents. He had some extra birthday money that his parents thought he should save. While at the bank Nate remembers being enthralled by the safe. It was large, imposing, and the door looked impressively secure. As a kid he thought and expected the bank to keep his deposited money under lock and key in that safe, tucked away in one of those little boxes on the wall. Imagine his surprise when his father told him the bank didn't store his money for him, but instead gave it to someone else! To say he was shocked would be an understatement. He gave his money to a bank to store and protect and here the bank was giving it away.

There are quite a few customers who would probably express the same shock that Nate had as a kid. Banks are viewed in the culture as a place to safely store money so it doesn't have to be stuffed under a mattress. This disconnect in expectations is one of the major reasons the Federal Deposit Insurance Corporation (FDIC) was created.

The FDIC was created in the early 1930s as a result of (bad) bank behavior and customer expectations. At that time banks operated with less capital and didn't restrict their investment activities to just lending.

For example, banks would engage in stock market speculation with deposits. When the stock market took a dive in the late 1920s customers panicked and realized that their "safe" deposits had vanished overnight in the stock market crash. Depositors lined up to withdraw their funds causing a nationwide "run on the bank". Banks didn't have enough cash on hand to give depositors their money back and many shuttered their doors leaving their depositors destitute.

The government stepped in and formed the FDIC, a government run deposit insurance corporation. After the creation of the FDIC depositors wouldn't have to worry about their deposits disappearing in stock market crashes or through bad investments on the part of their bank. The government would backstop all deposits up to a certain dollar limit. The dollar limit has changed through time and is currently $250,000 per account.

In exchange for creating and providing this insurance backstop the FDIC required a number of things of banks. The first is that banks must pay a fee to be a part of the FDIC. This fee is sized based on the amount of deposits a bank has and various other factors. The second is the FDIC required banks to become regulated entities and agree to additional oversight. No more could banks engage in wild stock market or real estate speculation, or operate with little to no capital. The FDIC would ensure that banks were well capitalized and weren't taking on excessive risk.

In a sense, the FDIC is the construct that permits a bank to engage in what seems to be two diametrically opposed functions. On the one hand, it guarantees customer deposits, but it also allows a bank to make loans with those deposits, which is an activity that inherently entails risk. The FDIC is the mechanism that allows a bank to borrow from depositors on a short-term basis and lend to borrowers on longer terms.

Deposit insurance also lowers the funding cost for banks. Depositors are willing to put money on deposit for a lower yield because their deposits are guaranteed by the FDIC. Depositors know that in the event of a bank failure they will be made whole.

Deposit insurance is a bank's competitive advantage. There are other financial service companies that engage in lending, but they're at a stark disadvantage to banks. This is because a bank can utilize low cost funding in the form of government guaranteed deposits whereas non-bank financial service companies that lend need to obtain financing through the debt markets, or raise funds via equity sales. Both of these methods of funding bear a much higher cost compared to deposits, and in turn require non-bank financial companies to lend at higher rates to cover their costs and make a profit.

While a bank's deposits are a competitive advantage, not all deposits are created equal. The easiest deposits to gather are the ones with the highest rates (i.e. "hot money", etc.), the hardest to acquire carry the lowest rates.

The lowest cost deposits for a bank are personal checking accounts or business checking accounts. Typically, checking account deposits don't pay any interest, but they are not "sticky" either as they are intended to be daily use accounts by account holders. Holders receive cash from their pay checks or revenue from their businesses, and then use those funds to pay for daily needs such as groceries, gas, or other bills. Checking accounts fluctuate daily as funds are deposited or withdrawn.

In the aggregate, a bank can rely on an average level of checking deposits over a given period of time. Checking accounts are both a blessing and a curse. They are the cheapest form of funding with their only real cost being either a minuscule amount of interest or the operational costs of supporting accounts. But they're a curse as well because in a recession or time of crisis these are the first funds to be drained from a bank.

Savings deposits are more steady, but also more expensive for a bank. Savings accounts are accounts where depositors can place money that isn't needed in the short term. Banks usually pay some interest on these accounts, but not as much as longer term deposits. Customers can withdraw from savings accounts at any time, although there is often a limitation on the number of transfers that may be made per month.

Most banks also set minimums for their savings accounts. Customers are required to keep a minimum balance in the account or they're charged service fees. Some banks go a step further and only pay interest at certain thresholds. For example a customer's first $10,000 might earn 0.5%, the next $10,000 might earn 0.75%, the next $10,000 might earn 1%, and so on.

The most costly type of deposit for a bank is a certificate of deposit (CD). A CD is a fixed duration instrument with a set yield. For example, a CD might mature in a year and pay 0.75% in interest. The bank is guaranteed the use of this money for a year and a customer either forfeits much of the interest due them or pays a penalty if they want to withdraw the money from the CD early.

When a bank relies on CD funding they are accepting a higher funding cost for duration certainty. Another reason banks gravitate towards CD funding is because it's easier. In business it is always easier to compete on price rather than value. It's easier for a bank to hang a shingle and offer CDs that pay a 0.25% higher interest rate compared to working on their customer service, their product offerings, or providing the best products at attractive rates. Instead of working to improve core business failings many banks take the easy way out and sell CDs at slightly higher yields. It's a terrible bargain, but in a culture when "I'll start Monday" is the diet mantra it's really no surprise that bankers are hesitant to get their hands dirty and rock the boat of their business.

A CD sold by the bank itself doesn't earn the reward for being the deposit with the highest cost. That title goes to brokered CDs. Brokered deposits are one of those things that no banker will readily admit to relying on, but many do. Bankers will loudly proclaim that their core deposit franchise is strong and they don't need to rely on high cost brokered deposits, but when one looks at financial statements they often tell a much different story. Brokered deposits are a way of life for many banks.

What exactly are brokered deposits? They're CDs sold by third party broker networks to customers that have no relationship to the bank. To a customer, a bank's CD offering is one of hundreds in a list on their brokerage screen. All the customer cares about is purchasing the highest yielding product. Brokered CDs become a game of yield. Banks that want to acquire deposits quickly need to offer the highest yielding CDs and continually do so.

The problem with brokered deposits is two-fold. The first issue is they are the highest cost deposits available to a bank. Every basis point of yield a bank gives up on deposits they need to make back on either their loan pricing or by more efficient operations. Since lending is mostly a commodity business with competitive yields it leaves banks trying to make up the difference through more efficient operations. This is something most banks have trouble with, especially those banks that are willing to take brokered CDs at virtually any cost for funding. When a bank takes on additional funding cost it's unlikely that they'll be able to find other places to make up the difference. The net is that brokered CDs eat directly into a bank's profit.

The second issue with brokered deposits is that customers with these types of products have no loyalty to the bank. In this age of technology customer loyalty is on a decline, but it's still real. When a customer ties their direct deposit into a checking account and hooks their bills into the same account they have effectively tied their financial life to a given bank. It's very hard for most people to move banks without significant inconvenience or financial disruption. Even a bank's customers with money on deposit in higher cost CDs have a sense of loyalty that a non-local customer who purchases a brokered CD doesn't have. The lack of loyalty and competition on price means that if a bank doesn't continually offer the highest yield then few of their brokered CD customers will stay with them when their CD rolls over. Why would they? They're entire reason for purchasing the CD is a high yield.

Deposits can be a source of a bank's competitive advantage. Every bank relies on deposits for funding, but banks that can maximize their deposit structure, grow deposits, keep costs low and retain customers are a step or two ahead of other banks. A bank's deposits are a very powerful profitability lever that banks can use.

Practically speaking you're probably wondering how a bank can gain a competitive advantage through deposits. It can be achieved in a number of ways. There are currently two significant ways to do this with business checking and with technology.

Traditionally the best source of funding for banks has been with business accounts. Business checking accounts are on average larger in size compared to retail checking accounts. But, there are other factors that make business checking the ideal funding platform.

When a bank extends a loan to a commercial borrower a condition of the loan is typically that the borrower keep a certain percentage of the loan in a non-interest bearing checking account. This ensures that the company will always have sufficient cash on hand to make payments. It also helps de-risk the loan for the bank. However, it can also provide another benefit.

A commercial borrower is required to keep cash in the bank even though they receive no interest on the funds. Yet, they pay interest on the loan they've taken. So, in essence, the business pays interest to have access to some of their own cash. Furthermore, these deposits can be used by the bank to support additional lending.

It's hard for a bank to fill their deposit coffers with just business checking accounts. So what's a bank to do if they want to attract low cost deposits without becoming a business bank? They employ technology to gather deposits and reduce their deposit cost.

In the world of smart phones, iPads and smart watches, most Americans are only a few inches away from a device that can be used to conduct banking transactions at all hours of the day. This is a new development, and one that savvy banks have taken advantage of. Historically, before Internet banking, a customer had to drive to a branch and have a bank teller physically process their weekly deposit. Bank branches would have special hours on Friday to accommodate the influx of paycheck deposits. Deposit gathering was personnel intensive as it required tellers and accountants to receive and clear the deposits. All of this changed with the tech revolution.

Now bank customers can have their paycheck directly deposited into a bank. They can transfer funds between accounts in seconds on their phone or computer. They can pay bills electronically, and checks can be deposited remotely via smart phone apps. The only bank employees involved in making sure this is possible are programmers and IT departments making sure the bank's servers are humming along without issue. There is no longer a need for tellers or even bank branches for that matter.

The role of a bank branch is transitioning from a place where customers interact directly with the bank on routine and mundane matters, to a place where higher value products, such as mortgages or investment products, are sold. Branch traffic is down across the board. One banker at a traditional savings bank (where higher traffic would be expected) mentioned to one of your authors that their branch traffic has dropped 75% with the advent of Internet banking.

When everything can be processed online a bank's branches have lost their value as a touch point for customers and have become an expensive line item on financial statements. It doesn't make sense to employ people to serve customers in a building that customers never frequent.

Banks have modified their deposit sales from a previous brick and mortar existence and moved it to the digital world. Banks now compete on the design and usability of their web app, not an additional 10bps of deposit interest. Banks that are growing and attracting deposits have integrated products allowing customers to easily manage their entire financial life online. Some banks have apps that allow customers to set savings goals or spending goals, or help them pay down credit card debt. All of these apps have features that are beneficial to customers, but don't require any additional employees. In most cases the apps allow banks to shed employees and simplify their cost structure.

An issue for investors evaluating a bank is to figure out where the bank is investing for future deposits. Banks that wish to lag their peers and fall behind are reinvesting in branches expecting them to fuel future growth. Banks that are forward thinking and have realized the industry winds have shifted are investing in technology.

So how should investors look at a bank's deposits? Like anything with banks, their deposits should be viewed in context. If one is looking at a bank that's selling at a very low multiple compared to peers, then having an inefficient deposit structure might not be so terrible (in that one is being compensated for it via a low price). But, in the context of what's "best" one wants to look for a bank with low cost deposits and a high percentage of non-interest bearing deposits.

Let's look at an example of two banks, one with an inefficient deposit structure and one with an efficient deposit structure.

In this example to make things easy let's assume both banks earn 4% on their loans. Bank A pays .5% for their deposits whereas Bank B is paying 1% on their deposits. The effect of this additional half a percentage can be shown below.

	Bank A	Bank B
Assets	10000	10000
Deposits	9000	9000
Interest received	400	400
Deposits		
Rate paid	0.50%	1%
Interest paid	45	90
Net interest	355	310
OpExpenses	250	250
Pre-tax income	105	60
Taxes	34.65	19.8
Net income	70	40
ROA	0.7%	0.4%

To a customer the difference between .5% on their deposits and 1% is small on an absolute level, yet to the bank paying these rates the difference in results is stark. A bank paying more for deposits will end up earning almost 50% less net income.

Of course there is one other way of obtaining deposits for a bank. Just buy them in the form of a branch purchase or by purchasing another bank outright. In the current world of low rates when the cost of money for a bank is almost zero it's questionable as to why a bank would need to purchase deposits from another bank.

Instead, most branches that are acquired for their deposits are done so by a bank looking to establish a foothold in a new market. It's much easier for a bank to purchase an existing and established branch in a new region compared to starting a branch without any existing customer relationships.

EVALUATING DEPOSITS

It's important to assess the quality of a bank's deposits. Unlike loans, however, there are not many deposit specific metrics that banks are evaluated on.

As we detailed earlier in the chapter a bank with an ideal deposit mixture should have little to no high cost brokered deposits and the majority of their deposits in low cost demand deposit accounts. Any sort of deposit with a maturity results in an additional expense for the bank.

A bank's deposit effectiveness can be evaluated in the context of what their deposits look like compared to local, regional and national peers. It's foolish to look for the "best" bank with the lowest cost deposits because there will always be just one. In addition, the bank with the lowest cost deposits, or the ideal deposit mixture, might have other unattractive attributes beyond their deposits. Rather, the investor should strive to find a bank with management that is aware that deposits are a crucial asset for the bank and has worked to keep deposit costs low. A bank with low cost deposits is a bank with a good brand. This blanket statement can be made because it's hard for banks with bad brands and reputations to attract deposits.

It's worth comparing the rates a bank is paying on their deposits with the FDIC deposit rate averages that are published weekly. The averages are available for free at the FDIC website, and banks prominently display their rates on their websites. One thing you might notice is the FDIC also publishes rate caps on deposits. The regulator determines what the absolute maximum yield a bank can pay on their deposits and publishes this rate. Typically, banks that are paying close to the rate cap are experiencing funding difficulties.

A bank's deposits provide a low cost source of funding and are a crucial asset that should be cultivated and nurtured. Too many banks view their deposits as a cost center, but deposits aren't the only expenses for a bank. A bank also has expenses related to acquiring and supporting their deposit base. This topic is explored in the next chapter.

11 EXPENSES AND NON-INTEREST INCOME

About this chapter something needs to be said upfront. If you were looking for the most unexciting chapter of the book you've found it. But for how pedestrian expenses and non-interest income are they do deserve to be covered in some level of detail. Instead of writing a comprehensive chapter of everything you might encounter in this category we want to focus on some of the important expense and non-interest income items, as well as provide a way to look at these when analyzing a bank.

EXPENSES

It is a certainty that a bank's expenses will consume the majority of their net interest income. All banks have expenses that are necessary to operate their business. Typically, the largest expense item will be the salaries paid to employees. In some ways just stating this is rehashing the obvious. Without people to run a bank, there is no bank. But, as the expression goes, the devil is in the details.

For any given task there are often different ways to accomplish it using either a few people or a lot of people. One can employ hundreds of laborers to dig a trench with their hands, sticks and shovels. Or, they can hire an excavator operated by a single person. The decision between these two employment models might rest on the cost or efficiency of each.

This same principle applies to bank operations. Some banks process all deposits and withdrawals manually with bank tellers, while others employ automated teller machines (ATMs) to digitally do the same work as human tellers. One model isn't necessarily better or worse, it depends on the bank and their business model.

If a given bank is centered around high-touch customer service built on relationships it might be appropriate for all banking transactions to require a human to complete them. Whereas, if a bank is operating an undifferentiated business model it makes sense for them to automate as much as possible to reduce personnel expense.

Where banks get in trouble is when their salary expense doesn't match their business model. For example, a bank catering to digitally-connected 9-5 employees doesn't need to have a full staff of tellers standing around waiting for non-existent customers during the business day. A bank with this type of clientele would be better served spending money on their IT operations and online banking so customers could bank themselves on their own time over a computer or smart phone.

There is no one size fits all rule for evaluating bank salary expense. The best way to determine if a bank is paying appropriately and is sized adequately is to compare the bank to state and local peers. An example is shown below of a bank's salary expense and their number of employees compared to state and local averages. This type of comparison analysis should be viewed within the context of the bank's business model. A bank should be staffed similarly to a large number of its peers unless their business model is truly unique and there is a reason for them to have more or fewer employees.

The best comparison for salaries is with local banking peers. This is because salaries are very regional and vary greatly depending on whether the bank is an urban, suburban or rural area. Even a state peer comparison could be extremely misleading. A community bank in Elmira, NY will not be paying their employees the same as a similar sized community bank located in New York City. Yet, a state peer comparison might group these two banks together, whereas a local peer comparison would not.

The second largest expense for most banks is their back office processing operations. This is a bank's core IT system, the system that runs all of the operations of the bank. There are a number of different vendors for the core system and their pricing is similar. The cost of the system increases as the size of the bank increases. It is not unusual for a small bank to be paying $500,000 or $1,000,000 per year for this system. Larger banks take back office processing a step further and bring these functions in house. This requires a full time IT staff of developers, systems administrators, analysts and management.

As a bank grows their IT spending grows along with it if the bank isn't stuck in a time that hasn't changed since Andy Griffith kept the good folk of Mayberry safe and secure. While a smaller bank is focused on reconciling transactions, a large bank will have a department focused on building and supporting software to deal with international wire transfers.

In addition to employee salaries and IT expenses, other operating expenses incidental to running a bank are typically things like energy bills, operating costs related to having a physical presence and other tangible items such as the toasters they give out to new depositors.

You might be wondering why we haven't discussed regulatory expenses. We have. Did you miss it? Regulatory compliance costs fall into two buckets: people to manage compliance and software systems to manage compliance. Banks don't typically report their spending directly related to regulatory compliance, but you can spot these expenses as they flow through other categories.

The overarching concept on bank expenses should be that no category of expense should be out of line with averages unless there is a very specific and known exception for it. If a bank is in the same business as competitors in the same region they should be similarly staffed and pay similar amounts, all things considered.

Non-Interest income

A bank's non-interest income can be a source of additional profits not predicated on the making of loans and an indicator that the bank might be able to generate revenue outside of traditional lending.

The easiest source of non-interest income to discuss is service fees and other banking related charges. When a bank charges a customer $1.50 to use a competitor's ATM the portion of that $1.50 that doesn't cover the network fees is booked as non-interest income. The same is true for overdraft fees, low balance fees and any other fee that a bank can dream up. As one commercial recently put it, sometimes there's even the "fee fee".

For years, service fees on accounts were a source of predictable and steady revenue. That is, until banks took it too far. In their quest for non-interest revenue some banks started to rig the overdraft system reordering credits from the smallest to the largest ensuring that a $3.50 Starbucks coffee would clear the account, but the rent check would bounce. Understandably, this behavior attracted the attention of regulators and the practice has been regulated and reduced.

While service fees have been curtailed, there are a number of other sources of non-interest income that aren't going to attract a regulator's attention in the same manner. The two largest sources are revenue from financial advisory services and revenue from affiliated companies.

Prior to the 1930s it wasn't uncommon for a bank to invest depositor money in equities. The Crash of 1929 and subsequent bank crisis ended this practice. Banks can still invest in equities on a very small level, but it is usually frowned upon by regulators to the point where often a regulator will force a sale of such securities upon discovery. While banks can't invest directly they can still advise their clients on how to invest.

This advice can take many different forms from simple retirement account planning to mutual fund recommendations to running their own funds. One of the largest banks in the US is State Street Bank, a trust bank that has custody of trillions in equity and bond assets for clients. State Street makes their money not by investing in the market directly, but by charging a small fee for holding client assets and instruments. State Street is the largest trust bank, but there are hundreds of other banks that specialize in managing assets for clients. In most cases it's a side business to their main lending income stream.

A second source of non-interest income is revenue from affiliated companies. Banks are not allowed to own other financial service companies, such as insurance companies or mortgage brokerages. However, bank holding companies are allowed to and the savvy ones diversify their revenue streams by doing so.

The most common type of financial service company for a bank holding company to own is one engaged financial advisory services. Financial advisory is an approved business activity for a bank and it fits well with banking. Bank customers are concerned about earning a return on their deposits over fixed intervals. Financial advisory is a product to help the customers earn a return over longer periods of time using products other than time deposits.

Another common type of business for a bank holding company to own is an insurance subsidiary. Insurance comes in a number of forms from title insurance to life insurance, and everything in between. A bank can use insurance as a cross-sell to current customers, especially business customers. "Looking for a loan today? Do you have Director insurance, or business insurance? We could extend a loan if you did, and we have an insurance subsidiary that could help you get these today."

There are a number of bank holding companies that own a variety of other real estate and financial service related companies such as mortgage brokers, title insurance companies, and other related businesses.

When analyzing a bank's expenses or non-interest income the same principle applies. There is usually one or two line items that dominate these categories, and those are the line items that need to be examined with a critical eye.

THE BANK INVESTORS HANDBOOK

12 CASH, ASSETS AND CAPITAL

Warren Zevon once put out a request (in song) for someone to send him lawyers, guns and money because the you know what had hit the fan. Bankers have a similar request (although likely not in a song), but it's for cash, assets and capital. Bankers have a love-hate relationship with regulatory capital. A certain amount is necessary to stay in business, but at some point too much holds them back from earning excess returns.

Would most banks prefer to operate with less rather than more capital? This isn't just an academic question as we know from history that given the opportunity banks will generally operate with the least amount of capital possible. Prior to the Great Financial Crisis there were banks with just a few percentage points of capital (compared to amount of assets) as if it was no big deal. Those bankers were either bailed out or have transitioned to telling war stories at the country club over adult beverages and a game of pinochle.

Banks are required to maintain certain levels of capital in order to meet regulatory requirements. The purpose of capital requirements is to act as a buffer against loss. The idea being that a bank should be able to withstand a certain amount of pain while remaining viable.

If you take a bank's assets and subtract all of their

liabilities, what's left over is their equity. To determine a bank's capital level in the most simplistic fashion (there are various wrinkles to it all) you divide the bank's equity by their total assets. For example, if a bank has $1,000 in equity and $10,000 in assets they would have a 10% capital ratio ($1,000/$10,000).

Regulators consider a bank with 8% in equity capital to be "well capitalized". But this 8% figure doesn't tell the whole story. There are many different components and types of capital. A bank has a core capital ratio, a Tier 1 ratio, a Tier 2 ratio and a total capital ratio. Beyond that, investors like to look at non-regulatory metrics such as equity to assets (E/A) or tangible equity to tangible assets (TE/TA).

All of these ratios and concepts can be confusing and trying to explain them runs the risk of providing a sleep aid which would make the dictionary look scintillating. Instead, let's take a step back and look at this from a more holistic perspective. This way equity and regulatory capital will begin to make sense without a deluge of terms and boring definitions.

As we've discussed, a bank's assets consist of everything from their cash, investment securities and loans to other miscellaneous items such as branches, officer life insurance policies and goodwill. Among these assets, as they say, cash is king. It's the most liquid asset which means that at any given time a bank can access and use it to fund anything from a customer withdrawal request to necessary operating expenses.

Think of the assets listed on the balance sheet as a ladder from the most liquid at the top to the most illiquid the further down you climb. Below cash there are investment securities, which includes everything from treasuries to corporate bonds to mortgage-backed securities. Then, there are loans ranging in duration from as little as a day or two to 30 years or more. See Chapter 9 for a more complete discussion of a bank's assets.

As noted, the primary reason a bank needs capital is to provide a buffer against risk. It's the institutional equivalent of a margin of safety. The safest bank is one that can withstand a severe credit disruption event or other shock to the system without impairing its business. This can only happen with sufficient capital.

One can loosely think of a bank's risk as something that's on a spectrum. At one end there is essentially no risk and at the other end is essentially pure risk. When mapped to capital levels – and perhaps more importantly for these purposes, types of capital – no risk would paired with 100% cash and pure risk would be with 100% of assets consisting of loans. A bank residing in the latter category would always be one day away from failure. They'd be the proverbial bank with one foot in the grave and the other on a banana peel. On the other hand, a bank in the 100% cash category would be safe but not earn enough money to stay in business.

Bankers look to maximize their return while regulators look to minimize risk. Between these two competing interests a balance exists where a bank can make a satisfactory return, while still minimizing as much risk as possible.

There are different elements to a bank's capital and different ways assets are counted towards capital. At the highest level a bank needs to have at least 8% of regulatory capital to be considered "well capitalized." Being "well capitalized" doesn't mean a bank is safe per se, it means the bank is above the minimum regulatory requirement for capital - nothing more, nothing less.

The second element of bank capital is determining what makes up that capital. This is a concept that can confuse novice bank investors. They divide a bank's equity into its assets in order to calculate what they believe is the appropriate capital ratio. The problem is this figure doesn't match the capital ratio that the FDIC calculates for the bank. Let's use the same example from above with a bank that has $10,000 in equity and $100,000 in assets and, therefore, a 10% equity ratio ($10,000/$100,000). The FDIC's calculation, however, called a Tier 1 or Tier 2 ratio, might be less, at say $8,000. Why is there a difference?

The way the FDIC examines capital is by assigning a risk rating to each asset. Assets are scored based on their risk level. Cash is taken at face value; a dollar of cash is worth a dollar of capital. Certain types of government securities are also considered safe and counted towards capital at face value. More generally, Tier 1 capital is a bank's equity and retained earnings.

There are other, sometimes intangible assets, that count towards equity in the accounting sense. These might be deferred tax assets or revaluation reserves. You can't liquidate a tax asset on a moment's notice to pay a depositor, and because of this these assets aren't valued at 100% of face value for capital purposes.

The job of a bank is to manage their capital in such a way as to maximize the potential for returns, while minimizing their risk profile. Some banks are too conservative and keep all of their non-loan assets in cash or Treasuries. This results in a high capital ratio, but low returns. Other banks try to skimp on safer assets and load up on riskier assets which (for a time anyway) can juice returns, but increases the risk profile of the bank, even if it meets the technical definition of "well capitalized".

It's appealing as an investor to outsource capital analysis to the regulators. After all, regulators earn their salary by examining banks regularly and ensuring that they're well capitalized. This is what they do. In most cases regulators find issues and instruct the applicable bank to correct them before they become serious. But regulators are human and are just as likely to make mistakes as anyone else.

Beyond mistakes regulators (and perhaps everyone else) may simply not be aware of a given risk. For example, there wasn't a proper appreciation of the risk by most for certain of the of the assets prevalent during the Great Financial Crisis such as a number of AAA rated securities that banks held as capital that weren't worth their face value in a crisis.

Some outsourcing to regulators can be done, but it always pays to double check the bank's balance sheet and build out your own risk profile rather than blindly relying on a regulator to do it for you. In Chapter 14 we'll take a deeper look at how to assess credit risk at a bank.

13 THE MANAGEMENT CHAPTER

If you do enough consulting work you'll eventually come away with a few observations. Every company believes their people are the greatest and that they work harder than anyone else. You'll also find that every company believes their culture is their secret sauce for success. It's an interesting observation because once you hear this enough you start to realize that everyone thinks they're the best and their culture is the best, even woefully underperforming companies or companies with significant culture/workplace issues.

It's true that a company's culture drives much of a company's business. But, it's also true that not everyone is the best. Simple statistics would tell us that most of us fall in the middle of the bell curve. We all like to think we're at the far right end with a house in Lake Wobegon, and maybe a few are, but the rest of us are squarely in the middle.

A lot of resources, money, brainpower, and energy has been wasted trying to find "the best" people for tasks. The problem is the best is usually taken already and is hard to pry away from whatever it is they're doing. In sports we see multi-million dollar contracts given to last year's top performers with no guarantee they'll continue to perform at that level in the future or with a different team.

The same thing happens in business. Formerly top performing CEOs are offered the sun and the moon. Sometimes it works. Sometimes the star comes in, changes everything and turns a lemon into an orange. But that's the unusual case. More often the success of the athlete or business executive came from a combination of their skills plus their team's or company's skills, not theirs alone. When you take someone out of a high performing environment their performance often suffers.

What does all this have to do with bank management? Great question. As you are well aware by now the vast majority of banks are commodity businesses with subtle competitive advantages related to their people and relationships. There are plenty of bad bankers who barely know an asset from a liability who are bumbling along. There are also excellent bank managers that are all stars. The gap between the truly terrible and the great isn't that large with much of what drives banking performance being not the people, but the business.

With approximately 6,000 banks in the US there are quite simply a lot of average banks. These average banks all earn average returns and have average business models. Plug in almost any manager to one of these institutions and the average performance will continue. This is almost by design, especially for a highly regulated industry. It's hard to be egregiously bad as the FDIC will come knocking. In addition, it's hard to be exceptionally good as there are too many regulatory barriers in place. Banking is an industry with a giant swath of average banks and a handful of outliers that are better and worse.

Yet, there is a paradox, much on a poor performing sports team. There is always a baseball team in dead last, but the players on that team don't conspire at the beginning of the year and decide "we want to be the worst." They are probably playing their best, but as a team can't make any progress. The same is true of banking. Average and below average managers didn't decide they want to operate a poorly performing bank. But, much like the poor performing baseball team it's a confluence of characters and events that results in poor performance.

There is a line of reasoning to the effect that by evaluating management personalities and characteristics one can identify above average management. And that, likewise, one should be able to identify below average management as well.

Your authors believe differently. We believe that the numbers are the ultimate grade for management. Regardless of what others might say about a management team, it's their bank's results that are the determining factor as to their quality.

This idea that the numbers tell the story is hotly contested. A common counterpoint is that maybe great management was stuck with a bad bank or a bad set of circumstances. But, there is a fallacy to this thinking. Great management is flexible and is able to handle bad circumstances, such as a poorly performing bank.

In one sense evaluating a bank's management is as simple as looking at their past results. How has the bank performed under a variety of scenarios? If the bank has performed well even under adverse scenarios then it's safe to presume that competent management is running the bank. If the bank has grown and thrived under a variety of economic scenarios then it's a safe conclusion that the bank has excellent management.

The biggest risk to a bank regarding management is when a bank has a new management team, or when a bank transitions from a trusted senior team to a new junior team. It's impossible to know the future and how people will react once placed in a position of power. The best guide is by looking at how the current team runs the company and their approach to succession. If management is egotistical and believes they are God's gift to mankind, then investors should be concerned with a transition. However, if a management team recognizes their flaws and is willing to promote people with superior skills - not just yes men - then a transition should be smooth. The worst management transitions are when someone rises to power in a domineering and aggressive way.

The last litmus test for management quality is how does the management team treat shareholders? Does the executive team treat shareholders as partners in the business? Or, like barnacles on the underside of a boat and an annoying attachment they need to deal with?

If a bank's management is showing good operating results and has exhibited shareholder friendly behavior, then an approving grade can be given and the investor can move on in their analysis. Too many investors get caught up in trying to analyze personalities. At some point it becomes entertainment and not much different than someone trying to analyze personalities on tv show, *The Bachelor*. True analysis can be done to contestants on *The Bachelor*, but the analysis won't result in anything meaningful. The same is true for bank management. At a certain point any additional analysis is just spinning wheels and entertainment.

The quality of a bank's management can be evaluated through their results. High quality managers produce high quality results. Low quality managers produce low quality results. A management team might speak like a high quality team, but if they produce low quality results quarter after quarter and year after year, they are a low quality team.

14 ASSESSING CREDIT RISK

This chapter provides some additional discussion on credit risk in addition to that provided in Chapters 10 and 12.

The very idea of analyzing credit risk is enough to give most investors pause and turn them off from ever looking at banks. Credit analysis is like the boogeyman in a horror movie. Investors are terrified to look in the closet, but if they did they'd discover in most cases it's just some big galoot in what used to be referred to as a dime store mask and lots of caked on makeup. We're going to break it down into easy, bite-sized steps and work logically to understand exactly what credit analysis is and what it means.

At the most basic level a determination of a bank's credit risk is really a determination of how likely it is that a bank will enter FDIC receivership or become insolvent. For the most part, credit risk is borne out of the risk a bank takes when making loans. A bank whose financial assets consist of cash and no loans has essentially zero credit risk. However, this bank does run the risk of becoming insolvent if they can't earn more than their expenses. They will effectively be a melting ice cube, a company drifting slowly towards zero. Safe, melting ice cubes are rare in banking. Most melting ice cubes have credit issues too.

As we discussed previously, risk can be viewed on a spectrum or continuum. Banks look to maximize their return for the least amount of risk incurred. The job of the bank investor is to determine whether a bank has marched too far past the tipping point in the balance between risk and reward.

In banking, the ramifications of excess risk taking don't always manifest themselves instantly. Typically, excess risk taking is uncovered, but sometimes it takes a complete business cycle before it becomes fully apparent. It's worth a brief mention that sometimes a bank gets lucky and never has to pay the piper. For example, leading up to the Great Financial Crisis many banks took excessive risks and were eventually bailed out by the US Government.

Opinions vary on how much credit analysis is sufficient. It ranges from the idea that one single metric can capture the riskiness of a bank to the view that a complex spreadsheet requiring a rocket scientist to operate is necessary. While a simple metric might be a good indicator of various things it doesn't (and can't) fully capture what's necessary to assess credit risk at a bank. On the other hand, complex spreadsheets give analysts a sense of false precision and lead to death by numbers. Thankfully, there's a middle ground where a few metrics combined with some simple formulas can provide an accurate view of a bank's credit risk.

The types of financial assets a bank owns can be broadly broken down into two categories: loans and investment securities. For all practical purposes – and certainly for purposes of this discussion - the cash a bank holds has no credit risk.

Banks prefer to earn a return on their funds when possible and most invest excess cash into investment securities. These securities can on occasion run into impairment issues and should be evaluated in a similar fashion to loans.

Investment securities fall into two general buckets: government backed securities and non-government backed securities.

Government backed securities are considered 'safer' than non-government backed securities. In turn, they trade with lower yields since there is a guarantee (explicit or implicit) that if the issuing institution runs into difficulties that the government will make creditors whole.

Non-government backed securities include instruments such as mortgage-backed securities or collateralized mortgage obligations. These are pools of mortgages bundled together to back a single security. They offer a bank the potential to earn a higher yield compared to government backed securities without originating the underlying loans themselves.

The best measure of credit risk in an investment portfolio is to look at how the bank's investment portfolio has performed historically. An investor should examine whether the bank's investment securities mixture has remained stable and, if it has, what their historical loss rates are per security type.

For example, if a bank has typically had 20% of their investment portfolio in mortgage-backed securities and those have historically had a 3% loss ratio then that portion of the portfolio could be expected to contribute 0.6% to the total loss ratio.

The larger concept related to investment securities is that banks get in trouble when they dip their toe into an area where they have little expertise. For example, if a bank has consistently held 80% of their non-loan assets in cash and invested the other 20% in Treasury securities an investor should be concerned if they suddenly are investing 50% of their capital in collateralized loan obligations.

Fortunately for bank investors, other than an outlier case here and there, investment securities are not the primary risk issue for a bank. The primary risk factor is the bank's own lending. Thankfully, credit analysis for outside investors is easier in this area.

Credit risk can be detected primarily through a few metrics related to a bank's non-performing assets (NPAs) and non-performing loans (NPLs). A NPL is typically a loan that is not performing pursuant to its terms following a given grace period. NPAs is an aggregate figure that includes NPLs, but also includes real estate the bank owns, usually obtained through foreclosure. Loans that are past due and non-performing are an immediate credit risk to the bank.

For simplicity's sake, a loan typically becomes a NPL when the borrower has stopped making required payments for 90 days or more (there are other factors and a NPL can encompass different things, but a longer discussion is outside the scope of this book). It's important to note that designating a loan as non-performing doesn't mean that it's worthless. The market is often quick to make this leap just as it does when it assumes, for example, that a company that misses its earnings estimate by a penny is no longer "good". Some NPLs do in fact go to zero - most don't - but what they have in common is that all of them by definition are not performing as expected.

Banks publish the amount of their past due loans as

well as NPLs and NPAs in their quarterly Call Reports. A word to the wise, this information can sometimes be cumbersome to obtain and organize, but it's aggregated and available online at CompleteBankData.com. Whether you view it through the service or pull it yourself, it's well worth taking the time to do so and, more importantly, analyze the data.

Think of past due loans and NPLs as an early warning system for future potential problems. If a borrower starts to miss payments or make late payments for extended periods of time it is likely, or possible in any case, that they are experiencing some financial distress. It's conceivable of course that a borrower might have taken a trip to Europe (or gone abroad as they used to say) and neglected to pay their mortgage while they're gone, but that's the exception, not the rule. Especially in the age of online bill pay and smartphone apps that will pay your bills while singing you a lullaby, a past due loan often spells trouble.

When a loan becomes past due the bank commences a process to do what it can to bring the loan current. A bank might call the borrower and figure out what they can do to help them get current on their loan. Depending on the bank, this program may be undertaken with different levels of aggressiveness. It's not in the best interest of the borrower or the bank to have a foreclosure or default situation arise.

When a past due loan passes the 89 day mark it is usually re-classified as non-performing. When a loan becomes non-performing the bank begins the process of maximizing their recovery either via foreclosure of the property, repossession or through filing an involuntary petition for bankruptcy against the borrower. In most cases, the process of recovery is arduous – it's long, costly and ties up the bank's capital for an extended period of time.

If a bank ends up foreclosing on, or otherwise taking possession of, real estate backing a loan that property becomes "other real estate owned" (ORE or OREO) and is listed on the balance sheet as such. It then becomes the job of the bank to sell this real estate as quickly as possible in order to unlock the capital that was initially tied up in the loan (and is now tied up in property it owns).

If the bank ends up selling a piece of OREO for less than the value it's carried at on their books they will charge-off the difference between the two values. It's important to note that at the time a property becomes OREO it will have also been written down to what the bank believes is it's realizable value.

Banks will also charge-off other loans if they believe there is no recovery potential. For example, this might be done in a case where a credit card borrower defaults on a credit card loan. This is typically unsecured debt and even if it was secured, there would usually be nothing for a bank to recover since it was probably used for some fine trendy threads, bottle service at high end nightclubs and other miscellaneous "must-haves".

As an investor it's wise to look for banks with a non-performing assets to total assets (NPA/Assets) ratio below 3%. Under 3% the risk is usually manageable for a bank while over 3% it can start to get dicey. Keep in mind that even a weaker bank's capital is usually 5-6% of assets (while a stronger bank is usually at least in the 8-10% range), so in a scenario where all of their NPAs became worthless that wouldn't in and of itself push the bank into insolvency.

There is a bit of a hidden "saving grace" on a bank's

journey through the impaired asset process. Banks are required to reserve a portion of their income against future loan losses (called the "allowance for loan losses" (ALL) on the balance sheet), so even if all of their NPAs were eventually worthless the hit to capital may not be as draconian as it might seem (although in many cases, as noted below, the ALL is insufficient). This is a safeguard required by regulators to ensure that NPAs don't imperil a bank under normal operating circumstances. A metric tracked at CompleteBankData.com is a bank's ALL to NPAs. Many banks are under-reserved which means if there were low recovery amounts on all of their NPAs the bank's capital could potentially be depleted.

The appropriate level of ALL is what is known in the technical sense as a squishy concept. There is both a factual and judgment call to it. A bank that is seemingly under reserved may in fact follow that path because they believe not all of their NPAs will go bad (i.e. high recovery rates). For example, a bank could be working with a borrower and know that a favorable resolution on a certain NPA is forthcoming.

Smaller banks tend to err on the side of over reserving. They stash far more cash away than is necessary. This can result in a situation where a bank has significant reserves but little to no troubled assets to be reserved against. It harkens back to the discussion of the risk/reward continuum. Too much in reserves can seemingly reduce risk, but in reality might simply be dampening returns. However, in those situations a bank can reverse their unnecessary reserves which then flow through the income statement and accrue to the shareholder equity account. One thing to be wary of is a bank that inflates its reserves in order to act as the proverbial cookie jar and draw on it when a boost to income is necessary.

The first and most important thing to think about with respect to the credit risk analysis for a bank is to determine whether it is safe and viable today. One should take into account the things we've talked about related to their current ALL, NPLs and NPAs, and evaluate these items both on a stand alone basis and as against their capital. Can the bank's capital take a hit given their current level of bad loans? Does the bank have enough reserves to survive defaults and limited recovery on their bad loans?

Once the current safety of the bank is established then it's time to look at their loan and asset portfolio with an eye to trying to predict the future credit risk situation. Examining a bank's assets for future risk is worthless if the bank is currently on shaky footing.

The future safety of a bank is determined by pulling out your trusty crystal ball, rubbing your hands together and cracking your knuckles to warm up, and then gently placing them over the ball while whispering secret incantations. This really works – at least in the movies. Alas, in real life it's just you, a list of banks to analyze and your best judgment. It's important to keep in mind that no one can predict the future (well, almost no one, wink wink).

A bank's future safety is determined primarily by analyzing the state of their loan book. This is an area where many investors get lost in the weeds. Just because banks provide a significant amount of data on their loans, loan exposure and portfolio doesn't mean that investors can predict the future with certainty. This is where judgment and experience rear their heads, come home to roost or just come into play.

Beyond the risks inherent in a loan portfolio, banks are exposed to many of the same risks of any other business, such as the risk of recession. There are other risks too that a bank might not even be aware of until the risk manifests itself. For example, consider a bank that lent money in the Love Canal area of New York prior to toxic waste being discovered there. Such a bank would have been taking in deposits and lending against Love Canal homes. Once toxic waste was found the value of the homes in the area vanished – poof! like a magic trick - they didn't just go to zero, they went below zero. People in the area would have paid to leave if there was a willing "buyer". A bank with exposure to that market ended owning a pile of assets with no recovery value, a risk that was exposed virtually overnight.

The way for an investor to protect against exogenous risks at a bank is to simply own more than one bank. That's right, diversify not only among banks themselves, but among banks in different geographies and non-correlated areas of lending. This seems like such a simple concept, but in the day and age of investors concentrating in their one or two best ideas and considering a portfolio of more than five stocks as "too diversified," it bears repeating. Simple diversification across banks with exposure to different sectors and different geographies mitigates risk. Period. Full stop.

Some investors throw up their hands since the future is an unknown quantity. Sure, we don't know what will happen, but certain conclusions can be drawn from the present based on the facts and circumstances at hand. If a person is a big drinker who often drives after drinking, it's a fair prediction that it's only a matter of time before they either crash, earn themselves a DUI, or worse. Of course no one knows if and when that will happen, but if their present actions continue one of these conclusions is almost inevitable. That is, the odds are in its favor of it occurring. The same can be said for banking. If a bank is engaged in reckless behavior and their behavior doesn't change, the outcome is predictable.

Nothing works forever, but trends frequently continue until they can't anymore. This is perhaps an overly simplistic and obvious statement, but once on a given path inertia takes over. In the banking industry it's often easier for a bank to continue on the path it's on rather than hop over to another path and force bank-wide change. For example, a bank with a deteriorating loan portfolio would typically need to do something extraordinary in order to reverse the trend and improve lending. Sometimes nothing works other than time.

Future credit risk at a bank is determined in part by looking at the existing trends related to the loan portfolio and extrapolating them into the near-term future. It should be pointed out that extrapolations far into the future don't hold much predictive value, but in the near-term, outside of exceptional circumstances, current trends tend to continue until they're forced to change.

As we've noted, the biggest determinant of a bank's future credit situation is the composition of their loan portfolio. Every loan bears different risks (ignoring for purposes of this discussion that there are some typically smaller loans that are more or less homogeneous), but painting with a broad brush there are certain types of loans that have a higher probability of risk than others.

For example, construction loans have a higher risk of default as compared to commercial loans. This is due to the nature of the loans. A commercial loan is typically for an established business, one that in theory at least has customers, revenue and history. A construction loan, on the other hand, is a loan based on the future vision of a real estate developer. The developer might have customers lined up for the final project - or not. Within the distinction between these two types of loans lies the analytical nature of bank analysis. A construction loan to a residential developer with a pre-sold development is not as risky as a commercial loan to a business in an economically unstable area. There are general steps to assessing risk, but the rules are very flexible.

Looking at a bank's loan portfolio and the trend of their NPLs gives an investor a clue as to what the future might look like. Knowing what the future might hold is important, but what's even more important is assessing how management - those an investor has entrusted with running the bank - will act when faced with difficult business conditions.

How management has acted in the past is the best guide as to how they'll act in the future. If management stood still as the bank crumbled during the Great Financial Crisis, it's reasonable to assume that they'd do it again if the situation arose. If management has traditionally been proactive in the past to contain problem loans and control credit quality, it's likely they will continue to do so.

Management that acts, but slowly and late, is the most dangerous to a bank. They are like the person one step away from bankruptcy who finally declares they're done with debt. Problems don't happen overnight and management that is unaware or is unwilling to act until the situation is bleakest is ineffective at best and is most likely extremely harmful to the future of the bank.

Credit risk analysis would be a piece of cake if investors could take a formula, plug some numbers in and spit out a result. Unfortunately, it isn't that easy. The metrics we've discussed are a great shortcut, but there is no substitute for human analysis, experience and judgment.

INTRO TO NEXT SECTION

Up to this point in the book we've been discussing the basics of banking. How a bank works, how to understand financial statements, and how to think about risk. Think of this material as "the what." Going forward the rest of the book is about "how." How one takes the information in the previous chapters and puts it together.

The remainder of this book is focused on putting this information into action. Converting knowledge into dollars and cents, either through better investment decisions, or by avoiding investment mistakes.

There is a maxim that floats around the investment world that states that investment analysis is more an art than a science. This maxim attempts to capture the idea that investment analysis requires the human element, a sense of judgment and insight, and those factors can't be automated by a system.

Any investor who has ever run a crude screen knows that an art element to investing exists. Screens contain companies that have one-time gains that boost financial results for a quarter but aren't sustainable. Other times screens don't capture future developments, such as an accretive acquisition that will immediately boost future earnings. There is an art element involved, but without the right guideposts and road markers the art isn't possible.

15 BANK M&A

It's a fact. The United States is over banked. Although there are approximately 6,000 banks, the four largest banks have more than 60% deposit market share. What this means is that there are around 6,000 banks, excluding the four largest, fighting over about 40% of the deposit market.

Amazingly, at its peak in the 1980s the US had over 15,000 banks. While the banking system has grown dramatically in size, the number of banking institutions has shrunk by well over half and its highly unlikely that this trend will stop anytime soon.

There are various factors driving the trend to banks merging and/or acquiring other banks. Regulators have made it known that their preferred bank size is one with at least $1 billion in assets. This leaves close to 4,000 banks wondering what comes next.

On top of this regulatory push there is also an aging trend in banking. Aging in the sense that many bank executives are getting older. Thousands of bankers joined the ranks in the 1970s and 1980s when banking was peaking and it was considered to be a sexier career option than it is today. Where the stereotype in the technology industry is that all CEOs are under 30 and wear hoodies to work, the stereotype about CEOs in the banking industry is that all CEOs are 65 or older, wear cardigans and argyle socks and dream of retiring to the links in South Florida. As with many stereotypes, there is a lot of truth in these.

At the macro level, banking in the aggregate is growing at the rate of GDP growth plus inflation, although most of that growth is being swallowed up by the largest banks. This means if a bank (other than one of the largest) desires to grow they essentially need to expand in niche markets or steal away customers from competitors. However, customer switching costs are high in banking and it's not easy to get a client to switch from one bank to another.

Separate from any kind of relationship built up over the years (which, granted, is less than it was in the past), customers have their financial lives tied up with their bank. Everything from direct deposit to automatic bill pay is pre-set and seamless which, incidentally, is exactly why banks are happy to provide these services – many of them *gratis* – to tie up their customers.

It's much easier to buy an established financial institution rather than trying to steal away all of their customers. An acquiring bank buys all of the customers, deposits, loans and intangible relationships of the acquired bank. Relationships are very important in business banking. Business borrowers often view their banking relationship as being with their lending officer instead of the actual bank itself. This is because the lending officer is the one who knows the needs of the business, its management and employees and is in weekly contact with the company. If a lending officer moves banks they typically take their book of business with them to the new bank.

Finally, the last factor favoring acquisition over an all out war for customers is that banking is a very gentile industry. Bankers are staid and formal grey suits who respect the unwritten rules of conduct. It is considered to be in bad faith to engage in what could be construed as hostile activities and sling mud in public. In a business built on relationships one never wants to do anything that looks bad or could imperil customer relationships.

When all of these factors are mashed together the historic trend that has witnessed approximately 15,000 banks decline to around 6,000 makes perfect sense. Moreover, the same factors still exist and will continue to exist which means that those 6,000 banks might shrink down to say 3,000, or even 2,000 or less, at some point in the distant or perhaps not so distant future.

The structural factors that push banks to acquire, or be acquired, is a boon to investors. While obviously any company can be acquired, to the extent an investor is looking for – or hoping for – investments that have a good shot at being bought out, banks provide a fertile pool of ideas. The loneliest and most forgotten bank stock on the planet can provide a nice return to investors even if no one else ever discovers it when it decides to sell to a larger bank. Shareholders are either given stock in the larger institution or are cashed out, often at values far above the last trading price.

The M&A boom in banking has been a hot topic in the investment world since the financial crisis. It's important to understand that whether M&A activity is higher than normal or not that such activity in the market, in addition to the other factors we've discussed, is a natural reaction to the number of banks in existence and will likely continue until such number is reduced to a much smaller set. To state it another way, the M&A trend among banks isn't a result of the Great Financial Crisis, but is in part (along with the other factors noted), a continuing byproduct of the fact that we had 15,000 banks in the 1980s which was far too many for the market to support.

The easiest way to take advantage of the M&A banking trend is to purchase banks that are well positioned to be acquired, sit back and wait for them to show you the money. But wait, there's a problem with this. Out of the 6,000 banks in the US only about 1,000 of them trade in the public markets. The majority of the M&A boom is thus out of reach for public market investors.

Let's take a small diversion for a minute and discuss purchasing positions in non-traded banks. The first instinct of investors is to see if a bank trades with their broker. If a bank doesn't have a ticker or isn't readily available via the broker most conclude it probably isn't worth a second thought. However, there is an opportunity set for savvy investors in buying positions in private and/or not easily traded banks.

As we've discussed, banks, other than mutuals, are like any other corporate institution owned by shareholders. The shareholders can be anything from the founders that started the bank to hordes of anonymous shareholders from all walks of life. But where there are shares there is a way (and an opportunity!) for an investor to purchase those shares. To buy an investment position in a private bank requires a lot more research and, in many cases, personal interaction with the bank's management. It also involves the expectation that once purchased the block of shares will be hard, if not impossible, to sell, especially in a timely manner.

If an investor is interested in purchasing a stake in a private bank the first step is to research its financial condition. This can be done on CompleteBankData or via the FDIC's website. The same detailed financial information exists for both private and public banks. If the bank is in a satisfactory financial state, the next step for an interested investor is to contact bank management or a Board member and discuss the desire to become a shareholder. With a private bank, shareholders might be expected to provide advice or become involved with the bank's operations in some limited capacity. There might also be the expectation that the investor keep a certain amount of money on deposit.

Once an investor finds a private bank that is willing to accept their investment, purchasing shares is a simple and straightforward matter. Such purchase typically requires a larger amount of initial capital and some local relationship building, but the benefits can be far more rewarding as compared to ownership of shares in a public bank.

An investor in a private bank with a personal relationship with management might find it easier to influence the bank to sell or acquire another bank. If you want to be actively involved, a private bank investment might be the right avenue for you.

Ok, so that was an interesting diversion into private bank investments, but now let's return to investing with an eye towards capitalizing on the M&A trend with publicly traded banks. Should one aim to buy a likely acquirer or a likely acquired? By definition, those are the only two choices when approaching bank M&A (or any M&A for that matter). Investors hold strong opinions about which strategy is better, but why can't both work?

Buying banks that are likely acquisition targets is a relatively simple investment strategy. Most banks that are purchased have some combination of inefficient operations, a lack of scale and excess capital. In other words, these banks are like giant plump turkeys walking around just days before Thanksgiving clueless about what comes next. They are ripe for the plucking (or, for the vegetarian readers, think of these banks as low hanging fruit ripe for the picking).

Underperformance and inefficient operations in banking is something of an interesting phenomenon considering that banks are essentially commodity companies. In a general sense, every bank is in the same business of taking deposits and making loans. There is nothing "special" about banking; money is fungible. So how is it that among the approximately 6,000 banks in the US performance varies so dramatically? It not only varies dramatically among banks in the same cities, but even sometimes right across the street from each other. It would be like two McDonalds on opposite sides of the street with the same menus, yet one has a thriving business while the other has limited business. How can it be?

The answer lies in the culture and management of the business. There are business model tweaks that can help, but at its root the reasons a bank performs or doesn't is often due to management. Does management have the ability to make the tough decisions and push for growth? Or, are they happy to run in idle and let inertia take hold? This might come as a shock to you, but there are a number of banks managed by teams that don't have a firm grasp of fundamental finance, interest rate risk or even risk in general. Or . . . maybe it won't come as a shock!

An underperforming set of assets is most likely underperforming because of the management at the helm, not the assets themselves. The largest operating costs for a bank are employee expenses and back office IT expenses. Both of these costs are heavily duplicated in an acquisition. A bank's core IT system can handle double the transactions for a small incremental cost addition, not the cost of two systems. A merged bank doesn't need two CFOs, or two marketing directors, or two risk officers.

Banks that are inefficiently and poorly run are an opportunity for efficient and better run banks. When investing in a poorly run bank investors should look to buy stock at a significant discount to book value (ideally, tangible book value) or at a low earnings multiple. Poorly run banks don't deserve to trade at a premium to other banks, but they also don't necessarily deserve to trade at depressed valuations either. A poorly run bank with excess capital, but also excess costs and a management team that is willing to sell is very valuable. An acquiring bank can acquire assets on the cheap and growth at a discount.

When looking to purchase a bank below book value scout out banks with unsatisfactory management teams and impaired operations, not impaired assets. A bank with poor quality assets might deserve the valuation they trade at. After all, those assets might be marked down soon or additional capital needed.

Some investors can't stomach the idea of owning stocks of underperforming banks, even if they're trading at a steep discount. It causes them to lose sleep, fiddle with their stock portfolio and lose faith in the strategy. Thankfully for them there is another way to play the bank M&A trade by purchasing banks on the acquisition side of the equation.

The advantage to an acquirer is that they get to purchase something that can become valuable with a little tender loving care at a discounted price. For example, consider an acquirer purchasing a stereotypically underperforming and over-capitalized bank trading for less than its book value. The acquirer can often purchase this bank, including its assets, deposits, relationships and so forth, at a discount to their stated book value. They can strip out duplicative costs, such as core processing, executive and non-executive positions and overlapping physical branches.

Customers of an acquired bank are unlikely to leave unless the acquiring bank is egregiously bad and mismanaged. More often it's the case that customers of the acquired bank will be happy to stay on and bank with a larger institution that has more products, potentially better rates and a larger staff. It's interesting to note that while customers will typically not leave on their own for such benefits (due to switching costs and the like), they are happy to get them if they don't have to change anything to do so.

Acquiring banks get to double dip in that they can get an immediate boost to earnings by eliminating costs at the acquired bank. They then get a second boost when they put those savings plus excess capital to work by generating new loans. Wash, rinse and repeat and it can become a virtuous cycle.

Of course, for an investor the only way to benefit from bank M&A is by playing the game, as they say. This means either targeting underperforming cheap banks, or buying banks building dynasties. Either strategy works and it's simply a matter of finding one that fits your personality.

16 FINDING POTENTIAL M&A CANDIDATES

Once you're on board with the idea that bank M&A is a well stocked pool to fish in, the logical question is where to find banks that will be buyers and/or sellers. The short answer is that other than the largest of the large institutions, eventually all banks will be buyers or sellers, or both, at different times. But, that would be taking the easy way out and besides it's not actionable. It's like the weather person saying that we should have a nice day soon.

There are two ways of approaching this question – from an acquiring bank's viewpoint and from an acquired bank's viewpoint. Let's take the more straightforward one first. We should note too that this is not a valuation discussion.

It's relatively easy to create a stereotype of a bank that is likely to sell themselves. They have less than $1 billion in assets, they have an aging CEO and Board of Directors, they are facing regulatory headwinds and suffer from increased compliance costs. They haven't figured out the formula to grow in a low rate environment and management is burned out.

You'll notice that not many of these factors are quantitative and can be found by running screens. They're all qualitative aspects to a bank, but that being said, they're easily identifiable. The best way to find out if a bank fits this mold is to read their investor letters. Most bank executives who are burned out write letters like someone who is burned out (funny how that happens). They complain about compliance costs, the tough economy, the weak recovery, the headwinds, the tailwinds and so on and so forth. You can almost feel their exhaustion as you read their words. These guys are writing in order to be saved. They are dying for a savior to come along and save them and their assets.

The problem is there are some managers who write like this, but who are the type to go down with the ship. These are managers who maybe have last names that are the same as street names in their town or whose grandfather is the bank's namesake. They aren't selling to anyone. It will be up to the FDIC to pry the bank out of their cold, dead hands and many of these banks might just die right along with their deposit base.

There are other signs an investor needs to look for when evaluating a bank's potential for acquisition. Is management more concerned about the community, their legacy and history over shareholder value? One of a bank's purposes is to serve their community, but an obsession with their mission is a red flag from an investment standpoint. It's not the type of bank that will willingly sell. Frankly, it's not the type of bank that will strive to earn a reasonable return on their assets either.

Finding a bank that is ripe for sale with a management team that's warmed to the idea is more art then science. However, time is on the investor's side. After investing in a few purchase targets you'll get the hang of what to look for. The other side of the equation - finding empire builders - is a lot easier.

The best way to find acquiring banks is to look for banks that have acquired other banks in the past and been successful at it. Unless you're feeling lucky, one never wants to be an investor in a bank that's learning the M&A game for the first time. It might work out well, but why should shareholders potentially suffer? There are plenty of banks with excellent track records of acquisition that are available for purchase. The ideal acquisitive bank is one that has a history of buying formerly underperforming banks, implementing a new system, and squeezing out earnings and growth where it didn't exist in the past.

The best banks are ones that have processes and systems for everything they do. They can buy a branch, plug it into their system and turn on the profit faucet from deposits. There is no science to this, it's just that management has discovered a repeatable process and they are diligent in implementing it.

The way they do this varies from bank to bank. It might be cross-selling loans, increased product visibility or applications (mobile and web) that increase usage and act as a magnet to pull other accounts to the bank. Regardless of what it is, banks that have a repeatable process and a system are what we're looking for.

As an investor, the best part about finding these types of acquiring banks is that bank managers aren't restricted to publicly held banks for their acquisition targets. We investors have to buy shares through brokerages or, as discussed before, potentially through privately negotiated transactions (if you're brave and daring enough). But, banks don't have to worry about that. A bank that is looking for a suitable purchase can look at any other operating bank, both public and private, that might suit their needs.

There are two advantages to buying an acquiring bank. The first is the market rewards these banks as they implement their strategy. When a bank can buy $1 worth of earnings for $0.75 or less, it's hard to stop buying. As long as the bank is a prudent buyer earnings will continue to grow along with market share and the stock multiple. Growth is valued and rewarded in the market, and investors could see their shares appreciate nicely as well.

Just like banks that are serial acquirers and have a workable system an investor needs something similar. Spend some time looking at banks that have been acquired or are doing the acquiring and study their businesses. Then, build out a process for yourself that you can repeat. Once you have the basics it's simply a matter of working the process and being patient.

17 VALUE REALIZATION – CATALYSTS AND ACTIVISM

There is a saying that value is its own catalyst. The point being that if an asset becomes cheap enough the discount of the asset itself will become the catalyst needed for the asset to re-rate to a higher valuation.

In the days of yore investors used to buy stocks with the intent to hold them for years and collect dividends. As the average holding period for stocks has fallen from years to months to even minutes, investors of all stripes have become impatient. This short-termism has infected even the longest term investors. This short term thinking has been accentuated by the virtually instant access to stock quotes from basically anywhere in the world.

When an investor wants to buy something undervalued, but not wait for the market to naturally re-value the asset (i.e. because it's cheap), they need to search for a catalyst. A catalyst is some external event that will speed up the value creation process.

Catalysts can range from a retiring CEO, to an expansion strategy, to an acquisition, a new product launch, activist investor involvement, stock market up-listing and various other things. Investors (and often bank management) look to any number of these as hopefully providing the spark that will light a fire under the stock price. Of course, what we think will happen and what really happens in the market and with stock prices are two different things.

Sometimes the catalyst that investors expect to unlock value comes to pass and value is unlocked. However, there are other times when the catalyst fails to materialize or it does materialize and the market doesn't react the way investors expected. It's times like these that most investors have probably thought to themselves, "if only I ran the company, I could close the value gap."

In Chapter 6 we discussed the bank activist investing strategy. In short, this is a strategy where investors follow activists into bank stocks with the hope that the activist will push bank management to unlock value. What if you find a really attractive bank investment and there is no activist involved? Is there a way for an individual, or a fund that isn't focused on bank activism, to unlock value?

It might come as a surprise that most shareholders are silent and that management rarely if ever interacts with them. At small community banks management is generally appreciative if any shareholders come to the annual meeting. Annual meetings are a great first step to opening a dialog with management. The meeting is on the bank's time, at their location, and management has dedicated themselves to spending a portion of the day interacting with shareholders.

Annual meetings have a general rhythm to them. A short introduction, followed by a few statements about the condition of the business, and then possibly a prepared Chairman remark and the results of any outstanding shareholder votes for director or otherwise. After that it's Q&A time for shareholders. Management is open to questions during the Q&A (and, thus, the name), but at smaller banks it might be preferable to ask a question or two in front of whatever audience there is, but then discuss any nitty-gritty details and proposals with management members informally afterwards.

When talking to any bank management it's important, as they say, to keep in mind that it's easier to trap flies with honey rather than vinegar. People respond to politeness and friendly encounters, rather than gruff, aggressive proposals even if both methods communicate the same message. Remember too that many of these bank managers are older and formal. Many of them are the pillars of their community and – right or wrong – are used to being treated with a certain deference and level of respect.

After initial contact has been made it's appropriate for an investor to call management to discuss the condition of the bank and its outlook, as well as any future actions to be taken. The goal for the investor is to become someone management can rely on for advice. It's from this position that management will be open to investor proposals to unlock shareholder value. You don't want to create an us versus them scenario. But, sometimes that scenario can't be avoided.

At smaller, closely held banks it's likely that management will treat the bank as their own, even if they don't own a majority of the shares. This is problematic because management is charged with running the bank for the benefit of shareholders, not themselves. See above for management being treated with deference, respect and so forth.

If management of a bank is running it for themselves, you've tried to communicate what would be best for the bank and shareholders to no avail, and there are no professional activists in sight, it might be time to run for the Board yourself. Waging a proxy battle against a bank isn't rocket science, but more like black magic. The public at large sees a lot of hand waving, some smoke and then a result without knowing what steps took place to get the result.

This isn't a book on activism, but we'll take a short detour to discuss it for a few pages. This is because methods of activism aren't widely known, but they aren't a secret and should be common knowledge for all shareholders. At a minimum, even knowing what to do should empower shareholders even if they don't do it.

In all 50 states courts recognize outside minority shareholders as legal owners of a business. It doesn't matter if the company is traded or non-traded, public or private, shareholders have legal standing and legal rights in the eyes of the court. A Board of Directors is theoretically put in place by shareholders to manage the bank. The Board reports to shareholders and management reports to the Board. When everything is working as it should, this is a good system.

What happens when shareholders are missing in action is that the Board becomes beholden to bank management and stops looking out for and answering to shareholders. Sometimes the Board will be comprised of insiders with a token outside shareholder. Sometimes a Board is nominally "independent" until you learn that everyone on the Board is golfing buddies with the CEO and they're all members of the same country club. When the Board doesn't report to shareholders any longer it's necessary for shareholders to correct the situation by voting out incumbent Board members, as well as possibly running for the Board themselves.

To run for the Board a shareholder needs to obtain the company's bylaws to determine what specific steps are necessary to run. Banks don't provide bylaws regularly and it might surprise or shock the bank that someone is requesting them.

As a legal owner of the corporation shareholders have the legal right to records and information that is relevant to their investment. Every state affords shareholders this right. To take advantage of it write a nicely worded letter to the bank referencing the relevant state law, include proof that you're a valid shareholder and explaining what you want (copy of the bylaws, shareholder list, annual reports, and so on). Some banks might not provide the information immediately, but with some pressure and, if necessary, a letter on a law firm's letterhead, you should be able to get the job done.

Running for the Board can be done either in concert with the bank or as an activist against the bank. The easiest way to get a seat on the Board is to find a friendly bank (it will probably be private and local) that has a Director who is about to retire. Speak to management about your desire to be a member of the Board and discuss what skills and abilities you can bring to the table. Finally, expect that the bank will probably require that you keep a substantial amount of money on deposit, potentially $25,000 or more. The key to getting on a Board with a friendly bank is to make a lot of relationships and connections, put feelers out and talk to local bankers.

The more familiar route that investors will recognize is for an investor to nominate themselves to the Board and then attempt to convince shareholders to vote for them via letters and public pronouncements. It's costly to run a proxy battle for a Board seat for both the activist and the bank. But, it's not unreasonably costly and an investor with a few million dollars invested in banks, or a fund with say $10 million in assets, can easily afford to fund a proxy battle of this sort.

In some cases the bank won't want to put up a costly fight and will look to settle with the shareholder. This is the ideal scenario as it shows that management isn't willing to waste shareholder capital on a scorched earth type of battle. However, not all managers are willing to settle and some have a "go down with the ship" mentality. This will require the battling shareholder to be more stubborn and determined than the bank itself. Determination, reason and financial backing have a way of swaying the silent majority of shareholders.

Activism and Board changes hold the most potential for value realization, but they aren't the only way for value to be created. At times a bank can provide its own catalyst and for most bank investors these are the situations to identify and invest in.

Let's talk about two catalysts that are easy to identify and provide short-term gains. The first is a bank that formerly had asset quality issues and is actively working towards a resolution.

When a bank has had problem loans in the past they end up in a situation where they have two issues overhanging on their income statement. The first is the bank will have an elevated level of reserves due to the historic bad loans. The bank will be required to reserve at a high rate even if their loan quality is improving. The second thing is the bank will likely have a substantial portion of those troubled assets on their books under the other real estate owned (ORE or OREO) category.

The ideal situation for an investor is to find a bank that

has these two conditions, but has cleaned up their assets. If the bank's asset quality has improved then their reserves are going to become a surplus soon. When the bank dials back their loan loss reserves earnings will increase, sometimes dramatically.

The second factor is the troubled assets. As assets turn south the bank eventually gains control of them. These assets are then held at what the bank considers fair value. The catalyst here is when a bank has an oversized portion of their balance sheet dedicated to ORE and begins to sell it off.

Bank owned troubled assets aren't counted towards regulatory capital. But once the bank disposes of the asset and converts it to cash it can be applied towards capital requirements. This means that as assets are disposed of and converted to cash it gives the bank capital to grow their lending capacity, which in turn will result in increased earnings.

The second easy catalyst to identify is a bank with a large amount of deferred tax assets. When a bank loses money they likely have no tax obligation for that quarter or period of time. Incidentally, the government in its infinite generosity allows the bank to carry over the loss to offset a future gain. For example, if a bank loses $100 in Q1 and earns $125 in Q2, the Q1 loss is applied to Q2's taxable income and the bank only pays taxes on the excess $25 worth of income.

The bank's losses that are reserved for future quarters are considered deferred tax assets. It's an asset in the sense that it can offset future taxes in the future. If the size of a bank's deferred tax assets is too large and it's unlikely the bank will ever earn enough income to utilize all of them before they expire, the bank is required to write down the amount (called a "valuation allowance") and move them off the balance sheet.

Banks that have survived extreme crisis events usually come out on the other side with sizable deferred tax asset balances that have been moved off the balance sheet. This amount will be mentioned in the notes to the financials in the annual report. These become valuable when the bank starts to make money again and can utilize these tax assets in the future to offset the income stream.

When a bank recognizes previously written down deferred tax assets (via the income statement), the book value of a bank increases by the value of these assets. The act of a bank earning enough to recognize previously disregarded tax assets is value creating by leading to an increase in book value. An investor in a bank that previously was worth 105% of book value might now own a bank at 98% of book value with the deferred tax assets fully or partially recognized.

Besides the change in book value, deferred tax asset realization also provides a powerful signal to the market. It shows that the bank is confident enough in their income stream that they believe they'll be able to use these assets in the near term. It validates their net income as not one-time events, but as a reliable stream of future earnings.

Another type of catalyst is operating growth. Investors tend to think of investments in terms of Newton's First Law. An object at rest stays at rest and an object in motion tends to stay in motion. We could restate it. A company without growth will never grow and a company that's growing will never stop growing. Unfortunately for investors, Newton's First Law doesn't apply.

Companies experience growth (positive or negative) for

a variety of reasons. Just as no tree grows forever, no company grows forever either. The converse is true as well since a company without growth might not stay that way forever.

The most rewarded catalyst by the market is most certainly growth. Take a bank that has shrunk for years, hires a rock star lending team and begins to steal market share from competitors. Within a few quarters management will go from being perceived as people with their head in the sand to lauded experts. Stocks of no-growth companies that become growth companies are rocket ships. As an investor, all you can do is hang on and hope you don't get burned on lift-off or re-entry.

So how can a bank turn on the growth? The easiest way is by increasing their two biggest balance sheet items - loans and deposits.

Growing deposits is easy in theory. A former banker told a story of how his bank wanted to increase their lending and to do so needed a stronger deposit base. He said they made signs advertising CD rates a quarter of a point higher than all of the competing banks and plastered the neighborhood. He said there was a line of senior citizens out the door and onto the sidewalk waiting to purchase a new CD. The demand was so great they turned people away. The problem is, as we discussed earlier in Chapter 10 on deposits, these are low quality deposits. They are "hot money". The same depositors will run out the door the next time another bank has a "CD sale." Sticky, low cost deposits come from long-term relationships. These relationships aren't built from high yielding CDs or gimmicky deposit account tricks. They take time and effort to be successful.

Lending is similar to deposits in that non-commodity

residential lending is all relationship based. Business lending is relationship based to the extreme, to the point where a lending officer can take their book of business with them to a competing bank if they get a better offer. A lending officer's clients feel they are banking with them, not with the bank.

The way a bank turns on the growth engine is by hiring away star lending managers. These managers bring in quality business loans and associated low cost, sticky deposit relationships. Bank management that realizes this and acts on it can find talent and increase deposits and lending, and eventually earnings and book value. This is the type of growth the market loves.

As you can see, there are a variety of different catalysts that can turn a bank investment from something boring to something amazing. The great thing about catalysts is they take time to develop. Savvy investors who are paying attention can spot developing catalysts before the market rewards the results from said catalyst.

18 FINDING BANK INVESTMENTS

One of the goals of this book is to put tangible and actionable tools in your hand to find and analyze bank investments. It's now time to figure out how to find these banks.

As you've probably come to realize throughout this book, banks are a different type of financial animal. Analyzing banks requires its own language and a different financial world view. We haven't mentioned a bank's EBITDA yet because it's a pointless metric. Just like General Electric doesn't have a net interest margin, Wells Fargo doesn't have an EBITDA (at least not one that has any meaning whatsoever). Unfortunately for bank investors, this point has been lost on most data services. Google Finance won't let you search for companies with a net interest margin greater than 3%, or for banks with a low amount of non-performing assets, but they will include banks in screens where the metric is for all practical purposes inapplicable to banks.

The finance world ironically isn't built to handle banks outside of a few bank-specific data products. It's ironic because banking is the bedrock of the finance industry, yet banks themselves are excluded from easy to use tools.

One of the reasons Nate created CompleteBankData was to build powerful screening tools for banking specific data sets. The software has the ability to screen based on bank specific characteristics and metrics that range from the broad (price to book, assets, deposits) to the very granular, such as FDIC loss sharing amounts. While Nate would love for every reader to subscribe to his software, he also knows that it isn't a reasonable expectation. While CompleteBankData's tools are extremely powerful and greatly simplify the research process, they aren't appropriate for everyone.

If you don't have access to CompleteBankData or another data provider, then the best place to start is anywhere you can get a list of bank names and ticker symbols. From a data provider work through the list and put together basic details such as the bank's market cap, their assets and their earnings. From this list you should start to spot outliers that are worth further investigation. Begin your review with the bank's call report, which is their regulatory financial data that is filed quarterly with the FDIC. The reports contain everything you need to begin your analysis.

If you aren't the type that likes to look through lists of banks, another place to find new bank ideas is on an idea generation site such as Seeking Alpha, SumZero or Value Investors Club (the last two are sites for members only). On any of these sites investors contribute investment theses on banks they consider to be undervalued. Don't take the write-ups at face value, but use them as a starting point to see whether a bank really is undervalued or not Make sure you do your own homework.

Sometimes ideas come about serendipitously through word of mouth, newspaper articles, blog posts, or by meeting a banker at a happy hour. Take any and all ideas and research them yourself, don't ever blindly take anyone's advice on an investment. They aren't responsible for your money - you are. Don't fall into a trap of outsourcing your thinking to someone else unless you've outsourced the entire process, such as with a financial advisor or an investment manager.

A last resource for idea generation is to look locally. Take a drive around your area and make note of the banks that have branches. Then, look and see if these banks are publicly traded or not. It isn't uncommon to find smaller community banks with a stock ticker and for those banks to be well run with prudent management and selling at a discount to fair value.

The best part about investing in a local bank is you can attend the annual shareholder meeting in person. Shareholder meetings can be an excellent venue to learn about how a bank's management views their business and their strategy. A bonus is most shareholder meetings are sparsely attended and you'll have management's ear for most of the meeting. Banks love to have local investors; building these relationships is easy by attending shareholder meetings.

If you don't have access to a powerful bank specific data provider such as CompleteBankData, then the legwork of finding bank investments will be somewhat more difficult. But, you'll find that once you start to develop some simple, repeatable habits you'll start to uncover ideas in no time. The difficulty isn't finding a potential bank investment idea, it's verifying that it's a good idea and that the bank is undervalued and worth an investment. And, that's the topic of the next – and final - chapter.

19 PUTTING IT ALL TOGETHER: A BANK INVESTING FRAMEWORK

If this book were a movie this would be the climax, the moment the audience is hanging on the edge of their seat for. If you skipped straight to this chapter you will be sorely disappointed, and probably a bit confused. At this point most business books try to please their readers by falling into the movie trap and wrapping everything up into a nice and neat package that has a "happily ever after" ending.

Unfortunately, the real world isn't like that. In the real world we're left to clean up the mess from the superheroes that threw busses and cars across town in an effort to capture the bad guy. The thing is we really didn't want to do this to you. We tried really hard to think of a slick acronym that used the word BANK or MONEY to represent some grand investment framework that is guaranteed to make you rich (or richer). But, we just aren't that creative. Instead, we're going to help you navigate the mess of the real world and apply all you've learned so far to analyzing banks as investments.

The first thing to keep in mind is that there is no magic formula. There is no secret method that can be programmed into a computer to print money. Formulas and rules work except for the exceptions, and it's the exceptions that lose you money. Instead of building a formula that ignores these exceptions, we embrace them. In the exceptions are opportunities to find hidden value that the market has missed.

Investors can be broadly grouped into two categories: those who believe in efficient markets and those that don't. There are few investors who acknowledge that the market is mostly efficient, but sometimes gets it wrong. One thing we've noticed at CompleteBankData is that on average the market is more right than wrong about valuing banks. In our software we have a function that values a bank given a standard set of assumptions, relative value, acquisition value, and a discounted dividend model. We take the average of these three values and call it "fair value." The amazing thing is most banks trade for fair value. If the model has a fair value of $32.71 the bank will usually be found trading for $31.87 or $33.02, right around fair value.

When the fact that most banks trade for roughly fair value is recognized one needs to consider why isn't a specific bank trading for their fair value? If the market is mostly right on average ,why are they wrong about a specific bank?

A mistake most beginning investors make is they presume that when there is a differential between a company's market price and fair value that the market is wrong and the company is cheap. This is incorrect, in many cases when a company trades for less than its fair value the market is still right. These companies have issues that if left unresolved leave the company with a deserved trading discount. If a bank has a management team that pays themselves egregiously and management owns a majority stake the bank shouldn't trade for the same multiple as a bank with shareholder friendly management that's intent on returning capital.

It's within this idea that the market is mostly right that we begin to look for bank investments. The first place to look is for a gap between a bank's fair value and their market value. A quick way to do this can be to screen for companies trading for a discount to their tangible book value, or at a low P/E ratio compared to peers. These metrics are simply a starting point to find these value gaps. A value gap itself doesn't mean anything other than it's a place that an investor needs to explore further.

Once a bank is found with a value gap the work begins. The overarching idea of our bank investing framework is that we're looking to confirm the market's view as quick as possible. This might seem like a strange approach, but it serves a few purposes.

If one accepts that the market mostly gets things right then the investor shouldn't spend their research time further confirming the market. Time is finite and it should be applied only to opportunities that are real, so any time spent researching or analyzing fairly valued companies is in a sense wasted time. There is no opportunity to make money in those names. The quicker an investor determines the market is right the quicker they can move on to the next opportunity.

One reason so many investors are hesitant to embrace this method is the fear of missing out. They're afraid that maybe they are missing something, and that they won't find another investment opportunity. There is good news though, of the over 1,000 listed banks there are always a few that are truly undervalued, and not undervalued because of asset issues, but undervalued because the market either doesn't understand them, or doesn't know they exist. Unless you have a desire to own hundreds of banks it will never be a problem finding five, ten, thirty or even fifty banks like this. When the pool is large and deep one should never fear moving their search to better waters.

The easiest way to find market confirming information regarding valuation gaps is to start searching where investors look first and expand from there. The most feared aspect of banking for the investment public at large is troubled loans and troubled assets.

The best place to start evaluating a bank is by looking at their troubled assets and non-performing loans. If a bank is trading at a discount and their asset quality is poor their discount is most likely justified. The key is to work through the worst asset issues first. As we discussed earlier in the book, a bank's asset quality trend is more important than the absolute level of their troubled assets. If a bank is showing quarter after quarter of asset quality deterioration, investors should be very wary.

It's important to differentiate between troubled assets and troubled loans. A troubled asset could range from foreclosed real estate owned by the bank to a bond in the bank's portfolio that's experiencing issues. Whereas, a troubled loan is a loan with issues. Banks with troubled lending outside of singular crisis scenarios should be avoided. These are banks that have a history of finding themselves in regulatory or capital situations that are of their own doing as a result of poor underwriting.

It should be emphasized that asset quality is paramount. As an outsider we don't have access to know or understand the details of a bank's troubled assets. What we do know is the level of troubled assets in relation to their capital and the trend of their troubled assets. Use history as a guide.

If a bank's asset quality is acceptable then it's time to

look at their loan portfolio. A bank's troubled assets show what's happening now, the bank's loan portfolio holds the key to what could happen in the future.

Different loan portfolio mixtures can result in different problems. If a bank dedicated 100% of their portfolio to construction loans then we could say the bank proverbially has one foot on a banana peel and the other in the grave. A risky loan mixture, or an outsized allocation to risky loans, might appear to be safe at the current moment, but it's only a matter of time before something happens and the bank runs into issues.

Investment manager David Merkel wrote a piece on his investment blog (http://www.alephblog.com) titled Bicycle Stability versus Table Stability. In the piece he explains that both a bicycle at speed and a table are stable items. However, for the bicycle to remain stable it needs to be continually propelled forward, whereas a table is by nature stable.

Banks exhibit both bicycle and table stability, but some banking business models rely more on the bicycle model than one might expect. When a bank is engaged in short term, high interest lending (consumer lending, auto lending, construction lending, short term business lending) they are in a continual pursuit of new borrowers as their old borrowers churn off. If the pie of new borrowers doesn't continually grow the bank will eventually find themselves in a situation where they need to compromise their lending standards to find growth.

When looking at a bank's loan portfolio ask yourself the question, "is this sustainable?" Is the bank's lending mixture sustainable in both good times and bad times? Even though residential lending isn't the highest yielding, it is a sustainable business model. Likewise, a bank that has a good mixture of residential and commercial, with a few dribs and drabs of other lending, is sustainable as well. It's when a bank capitalizes on a niche that an investor needs to conduct additional homework. Is the niche long lasting? Does the bank do something different in that niche?

When looking at a loan portfolio try to envision the types of ways the portfolio could cause the bank issues in the future.

Once you are satisfied that the bank's assets are acceptable and their loan portfolio isn't hiding any potential land mines, the next item of evaluation is the bank's capital. Some investors might argue that the first thing one should do is evaluate a bank's capital, but we disagree. A bank's capital is best viewed in light of their loans and asset quality. It's when those contexts are understood that a capital ratio makes sense.

First and foremost, a bank needs to be well capitalized. If a bank is operating just at or below the regulatory minimum extra caution should be taken when considering the investment. A regulatory minimum is just that, it's a minimum. The minimum is like getting a D- grade from a teacher. It's a passing grade, but just barely. Ideally, you want to find a bank that's well capitalized and is above the minimums with an additional buffer for loss. It's important that a bank doesn't go overboard with their capital. It's alright to be slightly over capitalized, but not grossly over capitalized. A bank should have an acceptable amount of regulatory capital, but also be efficient in their lending structure.

Banks with too little capital should be given extra time for investigation, but banks with too much capital should as well. A bank that has too much capital has an inefficient and lazy balance sheet and isn't maximizing their earnings. This is because too much cash is sitting on the sidelines and isn't being lent out and used to make a profit. A bank's purpose is to take insured deposits and invest those deposits into loans, not take deposits and invest them in a bond portfolio or simply hold them as cash.

Too much capital often indicates a bank that has trouble originating new loans. When a bank has trouble functioning in a core area it's a cause for concern.

Once these three checks are complete - assets, loans and capital - it's time to move on to the balance sheet and the income statement.

We evaluate the balance sheet first because this is the financial statement that drives the bank's earnings. The first item to analyze on a balance sheet is the bank's assets. A bank should have a pyramid structure to their assets with their loans forming the base and being the largest item. The next layer to the pyramid is investment securities. The amount of securities should be less than the loans, but more than cash on hand. Finally, the top of the pyramid is cash. When a bank doesn't have a pyramid with their assets they are either conducting business inefficiently, or non-traditionally. Neither of these are bad per se, but like any other issues encountered during analysis they require further investigation to see if they are warranted.

If the bank's assets are in-line with expectation then move on to their liabilities. When investigating liabilities you want to be evaluating if a bank has an efficient cost structure. To do this the first item to look for is preferred stock. When a bank is forced into a situation where they need to raise capital through preferred stock it's a sign that they don't have the strongest funding base. Preferred stock is a strong negative for a bank, but it can be counteracted with a low valuation. A bank trading near fair value with preferred stock should probably be avoided, but one trading at a steep discount to fair value with preferred stock might still be an attractive investment.

Preferred stock receives dividends before common stock. When calculating a bank's tangible book value subtract the value of their preferred stock. A common stock investor needs to see what the bank is worth if they were to pay off the preferred stock leaving only the common stock.

Another area of interest with the bank's liabilities is whether or not the bank has to rely on outside funding, such as FHLB loans or subordinated debt. The existence of subordinated debt or FHLB loans are another indication the bank doesn't have a strong deposit network. A bank taps into debt or FHLB lending when faced with growth they can't sustain with low cost deposits leaving them to rely on a higher cost source of funding. In some cases this is acceptable, but it needs to be viewed in context. A bank that has a history of debt or FHLB funding is one without a strong deposit base.

After reviewing asset quality, loans, capital, and the bank's balance sheet we finally move on to the income statement. Most investors look at a bank's earnings first and then other statements second, it at all. We look at the income statement last, because the balance sheet and other factors are of paramount importance.

Before diving into the income statement let's summarize where we're at. At this point we have found a bank that is trading for a discount to their fair value. They have acceptable assets, a loan portfolio that isn't hiding time bombs, adequate capital and a balance sheet with reasonable asset and liability management. We haven't found any reason for the bank to be trading for less than their fair value at this point. Our line of investigation continues to see if there anything lurking on the income statement that could justify a bank's fair value discount.

Because the majority of a bank's income statement is derived from their balance sheet there aren't many things to investigate that we haven't looked at otherwise. The largest items on the income statement we haven't seen at this point are non-interest expenses and non-interest income.

A bank's non-interest expense is all of the cost in running the bank, their employee salaries, their IT expenses, branch upkeep and anything else related to staying in business. Expenses should be similar to peer banks and other banks their size. There are very few tricks in banking to reduce expenses and, broadly, banks that are the same size have similar expense ratios. We are merely looking for similarities to average, because if our bank is similar in all respects to peers, except in their valuation, they should trade in line with peers as well.

A bank's non-interest income can be a source of additional income and could be derived from fees such as checking account fees, or from other lines of business such as asset management, insurance, or investment banking. Banks with high levels of non-interest income relative to their interest income can trade at higher multiples. But, there is also the potential for a bank with high non-interest income to trade at a discount if the market believes this revenue isn't sustainable or could come under regulatory scrutiny.

Outside of a bank's expenses look at a bank's income

statement relative to peers. A bank should have similar numbers to its peers of a similar size. If anything is out of line with peers then it could be a source of the bank's undervaluation. Otherwise, if a bank is in all respects similar to a peer institution they should have similar valuations.

Bank analysis is interesting in that there is a lot of supporting and financial data available for a bank, but not all of it is needed for each analysis. Bank analysis is like building a puzzle. At different points a piece of data might be needed to fill in the picture of what's happening. But not all puzzles are the same. When looking at one bank you might spend a lot of time analyzing the bank's cost structure, whereas with another you might spend a lot of time looking at the maturity and duration of their portfolio.

While there is a lot of supporting data, not all of it is needed in each analysis. Your time is precious, don't spend it looking at data that isn't necessary to reach a conclusion. If a bank has a history of low charge-offs and high quality underwriting with a low level of non-performing loans, it's not worth obsessing over a single foreclosed business or a few minor bad loans that are incidental. If your goal is to make money with bank stocks don't obsess over the minutia. If your goal is to make a career out of being a minutia expert then spend excessive time in the weeds, but know that your return won't come from investments, but rather your salary.

As we stated earlier in the chapter, the overarching goal in investigating a bank is to determine whether the value gap between the bank's fair value and their market value is justified. If you work your way through our framework and still can't justify the market value, then you've probably found an undervalued bank. The question is "what next?" The obvious answer is to buy the stock and wait. It's at this point that we can't offer much further advice because each portfolio is different. Some investors need to take liquidity into account, or only purchase stocks with dividends, or only listed stocks.

Regardless, if you have found an undervalued bank consider how that bank stock might fit in your portfolio and then purchase it and wait patiently until the bank stock appreciates to its fair value. And once that happens sell the shares and hunt for more!